Public Relations
Strategy

PR in Practice Series

**Published in association with the Chartered Institute of Public Relations
Series Editor: Anne Gregory**

Kogan Page has joined forces with the Chartered Institute of Public Relations to publish this unique series, which is designed specifically to meet the needs of the increasing numbers of people seeking to enter the public relations profession and the large band of existing PR professionals. Taking a practical, action-oriented approach, the books in the series concentrate on the day-to-day issues of public relations practice and management rather than academic history. They provide ideal primers for all those on CIPR, CAM and CIM courses or those taking NVQs in PR. For PR practitioners, they provide useful refreshers and ensure that their knowledge and skills are kept up to date.

Other titles in the series:

Creativity in Public Relations by Andy Green
Effective Internal Communication by Lyn Smith and Pamela Mounter
Effective Media Relations by Michael Bland, Alison Theaker and
    David Wragg
Effective Writing Skills for Public Relations by John Foster
Ethics in Public Relations by Patricia J Parsons
Managing Activism by Denise Deegan
Online Public Relations by David Phillips and Philip Young
Planning and Managing Public Relations Campaigns by Anne Gregory
Public Affairs in Practice by Stuart Thompson and Steve John
Public Relations: A practical guide to the basics by Philip Henslowe
Public Relations in Practice edited by Anne Gregory
Public Relations Strategy by Sandra Oliver
Risk Issues and Crisis Management in Public Relations by Michael Regester
    and Judy Larkin
Running a Public Relations Department by Mike Beard

The above titles are available from all good bookshops. To obtain further information, please go to the CIPR website (www.cipr.co.uk/books) or contact the publishers at the address below:

Kogan Page Ltd
120 Pentonville Road
London N1 9JN
Tel: 020 7278 0433   Fax: 020 7837 6348
www.koganpage.com

PR IN PRACTICE SERIES

Public Relations
Strategy

Third Edition

Sandra Oliver

KOGAN PAGE

London and Philadelphia

Publisher's note

Every possible effort has been made to ensure that the information contained in this book is accurate at the time of going to press, and the publishers and author cannot accept responsibility for any errors or omissions, however caused. No responsibility for loss or damage occasioned to any person acting, or refraining from action, as a result of the material in this publication can be accepted by the author, the editor, the publisher or any of the cited contributors.

First published in Great Britain and the United States in 2001 by Kogan Page Limited
Second edition, 2007
Third edition, 2010

120 Pentonville Road
London N1 9JN
United Kingdom
www.koganpage.com

525 South 4th Street, #241
Philadelphia PA 19147
USA

© Sandra Oliver, 2001, 2007, 2010

The right of Sandra Oliver to be identified as the author of this work has been asserted by her in accordance with the Copyright, Designs and Patents Act 1988.

ISBN 978 0 7494 5640 5

British Library Cataloguing-in-Publication Data

A CIP record for this book is available from the British Library.

Library of Congress Cataloging-in-Publication Data

Oliver, Sandra.
    Public relations strategy / Sandra Oliver.—3rd ed.
        p. cm.
    Includes bibliographical references and index.
    ISBN 978-0-7494-5640-5
    1. Public relations—Management. I. Title.
    HD59.O45 2010
    659.2–dc22
                                2009020214

Typeset by JS Typesetting Ltd, Porthcawl, Mid Glamorgan
Printed and bound in India by Replika Press Pvt Ltd

CONTENTS

List of Figures and Tables   vii
Foreword   ix
Preface   xi
Acknowledgements   xv

1. Not 'Just' Public Relations: PR strategy in a management
    context   1
    What is strategy? 2; Power and influence 4; Diktat vs dialogue 5;
    Public relations and organizational culture 6; Corporate
    communication academic models 6; Semantics 11; Operational
    strategy 15; The feedback cycle 20; Control vs co-dependency 21

2. PR's Place on the Board: A core governance role   27
    Costing communication 28; From function to strategy 31;
    Cognitive dissonance: coping with conflict 34; Ordinary PR
    management 35; Extraordinary PR management 35; Implications
    of ordinary and extraordinary management 37; The CEO as
    cultural icon 37; Performance assessment 39; Communicating
    risk 40; Reputation vs the operating and financial review 43;
    Strategic alliances 45; Crisis and resilience management 47; What
    the books say 50; Managerial perception 56; Corporate
    governance 58; Continuity planning 62

3. Reputation Management: A celebrity-driven society   **71**
Corporate image 72; Image and branding 73; Corporate
identity 74; Visual identity 75; Logos and livery: semiotics 76;
Substance vs style 77; Reputation indices 78

4. Internal Communication and PR: Employees as ambassadors   **87**
Mayhem vs morale 87; Privacy and confidentiality 88;
Communication as a core competency 88; Communicating
change 89; Change development plans 90; Fairness vs flexibility 91;
Communication as team effort 93

5. Beyond 'Customer is King': Sales and marketing promotion   **99**
Conceptual authenticity 100; Knowledge and skill 101;
Value-added 103; Competitive advantage 104; Customer
relations 107; Business-to-business relations 108; Web analysis
and evaluation 108; Efficiency vs effectiveness 110; Tools and
techniques 111; Marketing vs manufacturing 113

6. Media Relations: A borderless world view   **119**
Mass communication 119; Rhetoric vs reality 121; A note on
copyright 122; Message modelling 122; Think global, act local 124;
Media transparency 125; Face-to-face or Facebook? 125

7. Research Methods: Measures and motives   **131**
Art vs science 132; Validity and reliability 133; Balanced
scorecard 135; PR industry analysts 136; Grounded theory 137;
Narrative methods 138; Deconstruction guidelines 139; Reading
behaviour 140; Intertextuality analysis 144; PR as a social
science 146

8. The Ethical Dimension: A moral imperative   **153**
PR vs propaganda 154; Ethical evaluation 155

CIPR Code of Conduct   *167*
Online Sources   *169*
Bibliography   *171*
Index   *181*

LIST OF FIGURES AND TABLES

Figures

1.1	Factors influencing choice of model	7
1.2	The eight-factor PR integration model	9
1.3	Communication and the business continuity plan (BCP)	21
2.1	Factors in the choice of communication policy	30
2.2	Aligning communication leadership to corporate strategy	31
2.3	Stakeholder mapping matrix	32
2.4	The cultural web	33
2.5	PR performance indicators	39
2.6	Communicating the annual report	43
2.7	An operating and financial review (OFR) matrix	44
2.8	Overview of Philips' strategic alliances	46
2.9	Information costs and choices	57
2.10	Likely causes of crises before recession	58
2.11	A crisis impact model	62
2.12	Elements of a business continuity plan	63
2.13	Crisis and resilience: communication infrastructure	65
3.1	PR operational strategy process	78
3.2	Corporate reputation drivers	79
4.1	Three-phase communication change strategy	91

5.1	An integrated marketing communication (IMC) mix model	104
5.2	Basic sales and market intelligence	105
5.3	Target Group Index	106
5.4	A two-dimensional view of a web analysis page	109
5.5	A three-dimensional view of the same web analysis page	110
6.1	Perspectives on media and society	121
7.1	Content and method in early evaluation	132
7.2	Teleworking	135
7.3	Balanced scorecard application	136
7.4	Eyetracking the news – the Poynter study of print and online reading	142
7.5	A participant in the EyeTrack07 project	143
7.6	Historicity and social questions for intertextual analysis	145
7.7	Basic narrative themes	146
8.1	A framework for analysing strategic communication in the Poverty Reduction Strategy campaign	159

Tables

1.1	Dominant theoretical models	8
1.2	Key methods of data collection and methodological principles	12
1.3	Four traditional public relations models	17
1.4	Stakeholders' responsibilities	18
2.1	Communication in leadership	28
2.2	Importance of global leadership compared with other needs (based on a survey of US *Fortune 500* firms)	29
2.3	Operational PR functions in banks	48
2.4	Differences between routine emergencies and disasters	52
2.5	International terrorism incidents, 1968–79	53
2.6	Nine steps to managing BCP performance	63
3.1	A visual identity step model	75
3.2	Target audiences and PR messages, 'Leti'	83
5.1	Tool characteristics	112
5.2	Towards integration	113
8.1	Rational thinking vs generative thinking	157
8.2	Operational strategy, DPWN	164

FOREWORD

As public relations practice matures as an academic field of study, practitioners and scholars have come to recognise and articulate its strategic role. Not only is it a strategic discipline within organizations dealing with their relational, reputational and cultural assets, but the communicatively competent organization performs very differently from those that are not.

This book is aimed at public relations practitioners who already have some organizational experience. Its intention is to help practitioners consider their practice through a managerial lens. It introduces a range of theories and perspectives that link directly to public relations knowledge and awareness of empirical practice. One of the biggest and persistent criticisms of the public relations profession is that even many senior practitioners do not fully appreciate the management and behavioural context in which they operate. This book helps to remedy that shortcoming.

By also providing relevant case studies, the book is a most useful contribution to the growing body of public relations literature. It is particularly useful to both in-house and agency practitioners or consultants who offer strategic public relations advice, services and support. Although presented as an introductory text, it is not a light read. It requires the reader to engage in focused, reflective consideration of key strategic public relations concepts, such as alignment and integration, policy and planning. Getting to grips with these management concepts benefit personal and professional PR development, business innovation and overall communication skill.

Professor Anne Gregory, Series Editor

PREFACE

This book offers a glimpse into the proliferation of strategic management theories and models that have emerged to underpin public relations strategy in the last few years of e-commerce and the internet. Global expansion for industry and commerce has not only brought public relations management into sharp focus again but is clarifying context and status relative to other corporate priorities at any given time.

At the practical level, most in-house specialists are aware that they can carry out the tactical requirements demanded of them, such as media relations, trade shows and publicity events, internal and external publication production, including video, audio and film production, the annual report and other activities. Yet many struggle with main board directorates who, singly or collectively, ask questions that assume knowledge and appreciation of business strategy before appropriate responses are given and corporate public relations decisions made.

The ongoing intense debate about the nature versus the nurture of strategic public relations gets recycled with every new generation of PR students, particularly in respect of business and government communication versus propaganda, often referred to by the media as 'spin'. This inevitably puts added pressure on the public relations profession and the specialists who operate within it. However, all vocational disciplines have a private and public face to them and public relations, pivotal to corporate strategy, is no exception. Like management itself, the practice of strategic public relations is an art rather than a science. One thing is certain: e-commerce and the world wide web have changed not only the nature of a century's accumulated public relations theory and empirically based practice, but also the nurturing necessary for the next generation of managing practitioners, whether in-house (internal) or outsourced (external).

The global public relations industry is at a juncture of change and development where there is much confusion about the behavioural boundaries associated with its activities. While the academic subject of public relations is generally understood to be a management discipline for study purposes, many university departments around the world choose either not to identify with it as such or relegate it to being a subsidiary component of marketing, film or media studies. Of course, higher education generally is having to adapt to the information age and the complexities that this brings to all such interdisciplinary and multidisciplinary subjects, so to some extent the knowledge era offers new opportunities.

One issue that used to tax the minds of academics was that of public relations' comparability to other vocational disciplines such as accountancy or law in terms of its literature base and growing body of knowledge. Now, because universities have clear pathways with prescribed indicators to measure attainment in all disciplines, public relations education (knowledge) and training (skill) are assessed at each stage of the professional development process until specified learning outcomes are demonstrably achieved and any Chartered Institute of Public Relations (CIPR) accredited award can be given. In the acquisition of public relations management competencies, it is understood that today's students have proven conceptual understanding and tactical ability at both strategic and operational levels.

Any textbook claiming to represent a brief overview of public relations at advanced strategic level ought, by definition, to be able to assume that fundamental management concepts and mechanisms are understood and need not be reiterated. Suffice to say, that throughout the text the term 'public relations' is used as a noun and 'communication' its verb. Students of public relations, for example, will have proceeded from the CIPR Foundation Diploma level before attempting the qualifying CIPR Diploma, some of which concentrates on public relations strategy. New publications such as *PR Business* are emerging to meet a need, but often the best public relations students from both profit and not-for-profit organizations are those with a management background or those prepared to struggle with the prolificacy of management texts and viewpoints. For example, a corporate communications manager may act as deputy to the public relations director for all areas in a typical public relations department. While attempting to harmonize all communication through one department may sound sensible, but difficult to realize in practice, coordination has to be centralized somewhere, somehow. Role theory and other HR models such as group theory, provide the organization with straightforward human structures and processes for communication coordination to be properly integrated as PR management. A public relations department is and must remain strategic by definition, whether it provides one-off PR campaigns or a matrix of communication plans, outsources activities through PR agencies or employs advertising agencies, or uses management consultancies.

How far techniques can be included in any book on strategic public relations management raises some interesting questions about critical analysis, not least the negative perceptions of public relations as mere opportunism or publicity stunts. This book includes cases to assess tactics through discussion of real-world campaign summaries provided at the end of each chapter. The campaigns were all submitted to IPRA's Annual Golden World Award competition, and the outlines provided by those organizations offer an opportunity for deeper reflection to readers, students and practitioners alike. Typical issues for deeper consideration or discussion might include:

- key links between the chapter (theory) and the campaign (practice);
- any changes necessary to the campaigns to ensure 'best practice';
- what omissions appear to be revealed by the brief campaign narratives provided;
- what future research the campaigns indicate a need for, in 21st century public relations;
- within the bounds of the information provided, whether evaluation criteria appear to measure up empirically for quality assurance purposes;
- the way short-term event campaign results can potentially stabilize/ destabilize longer-term strategic planning cycles via their impact on other priorities or stakeholder group interests;
- how any immediate beneficial outcomes should be managed for reputation and its ongoing sustainability.

Thus the book begins by introducing readers to my empirical framework illustrating how the profession is organized through the functional, operational activities that make up each of eight specialist strategic areas. To the first or second jobber, this provides a focus for career guidance and continuous professional development (CPD). Some areas, such as events management, increasingly operate autonomously, albeit not always to CIPR regulatory standards, such is the proliferating demand for such services. This is a challenge for the public relations profession, which may increasingly find itself required to expand its education and enforcement role to retain public confidence and respect. As a consequence, this third edition replaces the Glossary with the CIPR Code of Conduct, which reiterates the best practice need for sound judgement at all times in the process of challenging everything we hear, see, say and do through the art of excellent communication that is the bedrock of sound, ethical PR practice.

ACKNOWLEDGEMENTS

I am grateful for permission to reproduce copyright material and all contributions are credited at source within the text. However, while every effort has been made to trace the owners of all copyright material, we offer apologies to any copyright holder whose rights may have unwittingly been infringed and welcome information that would enable us to contact them.

Special mention and grateful thanks must go to the companies featured in the updating of their material since the first edition in 2001; to the CIPR series editors for helpful comments; to Kogan Page for its support and translations of all editions; to member colleagues on the International Public Relations Association (IPRA) Golden World Award judging panel for their permission to include campaign entries; to postgraduate students from around the world studying on the Thames Valley University (TVU, London) CIPR-endorsed MSc Corporate Communication course, especially for the ever stimulating seminar debates; to that programme's Practitioner Panel whose professional input is always invaluable; to TVU tutors working together to encourage deep thinking and continuous professional development.

To my PR doctoral students whose work will help to sustain a better understood PR future; to the worldwide family of pure and applied researchers who attend the annual UK/US Corporate Communication Conference sponsored jointly by *Corporate Communication: An International Journal* and Corporate Communication International; to all the authors and analysts who have contributed and continue to contribute to the success of that leading academic research journal and the growing body of knowledge it represents.

Special thanks go Clare Cochrane, Wim Elving, Colin Farrington, Christina Genest, Michael Goodman, James Holt, Krystyna Kobiak, Sandra Macleod, Kunal Mehta, Antonio Grau Noguero, Colin Standfield, Kanwal Virdee, Gloria Walker, Reginald Watts and all friends and colleagues whose belief in the power and influence of sound communication to make a difference to the greater good – and development of the public relations industry itself – never fails to encourage and inspire.

1

NOT 'JUST' PUBLIC RELATIONS: PR strategy in a management context

When the Chartered Institute of Public Relations produced the results of its Delphi Survey a decade ago, the need for definition of the term 'public relations' (PR) was second to the measurement and evaluation of public relations in a hierarchy of research requirements as articulated by Institute members, both academic and practitioner. With any developing profession, reliable and valid research brings it to maturity. However, if definition is still a problem, theories, models, techniques and strategies remain abstract concepts. Or do they? Who can clearly define all types of accountancy, medicine or law in a single definitive statement?

Many organizations, though, are making a move away from the term 'public relations' towards corporate communication management in the naming of their restructured public relations and public affairs departments. Like the term 'management', public relations may rely more for its meaning when things go wrong than when things go right. Practitioners are well aware of the function of public relations and the techniques applied to carry out its commercial role in a business context. This chapter demonstrates how strategic public relations aligns itself to corporate strategy by involving an organization's full range of stakeholders. Before addressing this aspect, however, it is necessary to define what is meant by strategy.

What is strategy?

Over a decade ago J L Thompson (1995) defined strategy as a means to an end when he wrote, 'The ends concern the purposes and objectives of the organization. There is a broad strategy for the whole organization and a competitive strategy for each activity. Functional strategies contribute directly to competitive strategies.' Bennett (1996) described strategy as 'the direction that the organization chooses to follow in order to fulfil its mission'.

However, globalization has changed the face of managerial texts on the subject. Mintzberg *et al* (1998) offered five uses of the word 'strategy':

1. A plan as a consciously intended course of action.
2. A ploy as a specific manoeuvre intended to outwit an opponent or competitors.
3. A pattern representing a stream of actions.
4. A position as a means of locating an organization in an environment.
5. A perspective as an integrated way of perceiving the world.

Australian author Colin White (2004) offered a broad cognitive map by suggesting that three elements are prescriptive, namely strategy as design, planning and positioning, while 11 others describe what actually happens in strategy making. These become strategy as:

- entrepreneurship;
- the reflection of an organized culture or social web;
- a political process;
- a learning process;
- an episodic or transformative process;
- an expression of cognitive psychology;
- consisting in rhetoric or a language game;
- a reactive adaptation to environmental circumstances;
- an expression of ethics or as moral philosophy;
- the systematic application of rationality; and
- the use of simple rules.

White recognizes the central role that communication with stakeholders plays in strategic thinking and operations management. Today's generic models of strategy highlight four approaches:

1. classical (analyse, plan and command);
2. evolutionary (keeping costs low and options open);
3. processual (playing by the local rules);
4. systemic.

These all shadow the history of public relations (see also p 8), from classical through evolutionary and processual to the systemic model espoused in this book and others. These four dimensions include variables of power and culture, which many of the traditional models lacked. Inevitably, this is important in assessing the nature of organizational reality. For example, there would be a different emphasis in an organization driven by its investment stakeholders such as financiers, compared with an organization driven more by the community and local government or customers and suppliers.

The reflective in-house public relations practitioner does this in the normal course of his or her professional control activity and will be aware that:

- major public relations decisions influence organizational aims and objectives over time;
- public relations decisions involve a major commitment of resources;
- public relations decisions involve complex situations at corporate, business unit or other stakeholder levels that may affect or be affected by many parts of the organization; and
- executive public relations decisions are inevitably based on best available intelligence and sound knowledge management at the time and outcomes are transmuted into the longer-term decision-making cycle.

Although it differs from organization to organization, it is common practice for strategy making to take place at three levels, the macro or corporate, the micro or business unit and the individual/team or operational level. In small to medium-sized enterprises (SMEs), the business unit often operates at corporate level, whereas in the public sector, the UK's National Health Service (NHS) for example, strategic decisions are made from central government downwards, with operational strategies rolled out at local and regional level.

Whatever the structure, processes must be coherent and so communication strategies between various levels have to be consistent. There is often a lack of recognition of strategic decisions being made at different levels so the role of the public relations specialist is to ensure that consistency applies throughout; what UK politician Peter Mandelson referred to as being 'on message'. This did not mean 'common' or 'the same', although perception of the phrase was consistently changed by journalists and ministerial rivals to suggest that it did mean that. A basic understanding of managerial systems theory is crucial to all practitioners but, generally, the most pertinent theories used in public relations management can be summarized as follows.

Theories of relationships

- Systems theory, which evaluates relationships and structure as they relate to the whole.
- Situational theory, whereby situations define relationships.
- Approaches to conflict resolution, which include separating people from the problem; focusing on interests, not positions; inventing options for mutual gain; and insisting on objective criteria.

Theories of cognition and behaviour

- Action assembly theory is an aid to understanding behaviour by understanding how people think.
- Social exchange theory aims to predict behaviour of groups and individuals based on perceived rewards and costs.
- Diffusion theory, whereby people adopt an important idea or innovation after going through five discrete steps: awareness, interest, evaluation, trial and adoption.
- Social learning theory, whereby people use information processing to explain and predict behaviour.
- An elaborated likelihood model, which suggests that decision making is influenced through repetition, rewards and credible spokespersons.

Theories of mass communication

- Uses and gratification – people are active users of media and select media based on their gratification for them.
- Agenda-setting theory – suggests that media content that people read, see and listen to sets the agenda for society's discussion and interaction.

Probably the most common area of confusion by practitioners in respect of these theories is in the day-to-day management of brand image. Corporate brand image is as important as product brand image. Indeed, marketing uses many of the same channels of communication as those used in classic public relations and often the same media too. Both product branding and corporate image branding are concerned to move audiences from awareness to clearly defined perceptions that are seen to offer competitive or social advantage, but the underlying psychological tools and techniques will be different and subject to stakeholder analysis.

Power and influence

Because of its alignment with corporate strategy, strategic public relations incorporates power control models operating at the macro and micro levels, based around typical symmetrical models.

Most in-house practitioners know from experience that as advisers they rarely make final strategic business decisions or choices. This is usually made by the dominant coalition and thus, although all these factors may influence the choice of a model of strategic public relations, power control theory from organizational behaviour shows that the people who have power in an organization may choose the type of public relations programmes that they do for reasons best known to them. The traditional view of the in-house practitioner having a board appointment in order to better influence board decision making is only sustainable if the practitioner is highly skilled and experienced in environmental business management, organizational behaviour and interactive communication.

Diktat vs dialogue

Traditionally, diplomatic relations was seen as a branch of international relations for practising diplomats or other civil servants. In a contemporary, globalized world where industry and state are more closely bound than ever before, diplomacy becomes a critical skill in the public relations armoury of lobbying, negation, media relations, report writing, language and cultural analysis. Before the establishment of professional institutions such as the CIPR, diplomacy was 'public relations' – often unstated in university courses such as politics, philosophy and economics. The impact of globalization has added the term 'public diplomacy' to the worldwide lexicon in response to the way governments, countries and international organizations, such as businesses, charities and NGOs, communicate with each other. TV, the internet and telecommunication have captured people's interest and concerns for open dialogue, along with reactive/proactive resistance to propaganda, what some academics call the conflict between 'diktat and dialogue'.

The Vienna Convention on Diplomatic Relations lists Optional Protocols, and Article 2 clearly echoes the CIPR mission for 'mutual understanding' when it states that 'the establishment of diplomatic relations (between sexes) and of permanent diplomatic missions, takes place by mutual consent'. The Convention upholds the belief that diplomacy contributes to the development of friendly relations (among nations) irrespective of their differing constitutional and social systems.

This concept is in the spirit of best practice PR and comes into its own in corporate brand management and image building of organizations everywhere. So it is a dominant quality in a skilled PR practitioner. Management's conduct in exercising democratic power and influence can often come to depend on it.

Public relations and organizational culture

Organizational culture is created by the dominant coalition, especially by the founder or CEO of an organization, and public relations managers do not gain influence if their values and ideology differ substantially from that of the organization. Organizational culture is also affected by the larger societal culture and by the environment. It affects public relations in the long term by moulding the world view of the public relations function and thus influences the choice of a model of public relations within an organization; see Figure 1.1.

While such a model identifies many of the variables essential to communication management and control, it also shows that if a culture is essentially hierarchical, authoritarian and reactive, the dominant coalition will generally choose an asymmetrical model of public relations. Furthermore, it will choose not to be counselled by the public relations expert who traditionally was often not seen as having enough strategic awareness and therefore was of limited value. Many companies have changed their departmental names from 'public relations' to 'corporate communication' to reflect this development. With the future unknown, developmental debates centre on the dominant theoretical models I have identified; see Table 1.1.

Key day-to-day executive skills and technical expertise come together in professional practice to support public relations strategy in-house or outsourced to blue chip management consultancies and public relations agencies. In my eight-factor PR integration model shown in Figure 1.2, professional expertise is organized at micro (in-house relations) and macro (external relations) levels. Integrated communication tools and techniques can be broadly classified into eight strategic areas forming an integrated communication network. These have been defined as having a significant body of peer-reviewed knowledge underpinning them, based on academic theory and empirical research.

Corporate communication academic models

The study of corporate communication is perhaps one of the broadest multidisciplinary and interdisciplinary subjects available in universities today. Topics will be studied from:

- politics;
- economics;
- philosophy;
- languages, semiology and semantics;
- cultural studies;

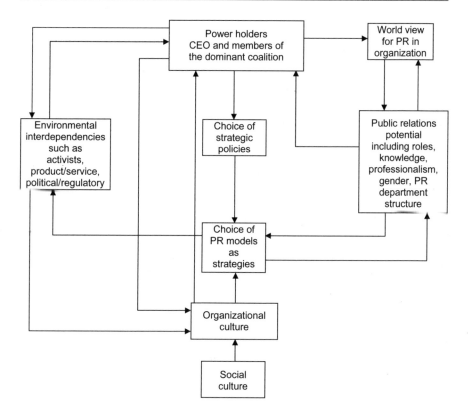

Source: Grunig (1992)

Key

The box labelled 'World view for PR in organization' assumes that public relations is dominant in an organization but, as the arrows show, the world view for public relations is, 'a product of the world view of the dominant coalition, the potential of the public relations department and the culture of the organization' (Grunig, 1992: 24). The arrow from environmental interdependencies to power holders indicates that, 'managers gain power when they have knowledge and skills that help organizations manage crucial environmental interdependencies'. The arrow from power holders to environmental interdependencies indicates that, 'the environment is in part at least the subjective perception of the dominant coalition'. The arrow from the choice of public relations models as strategies to the environment, 'depicts the critical relationship between strategic management of public relations and organizational effectiveness'. The final two boxes, 'depict the relationship among societal culture, organizational culture and excellence in public relations'.

Figure 1.1 *Factors influencing choice of model*

Table 1.1 *Dominant theoretical models*

Selected characteristics	Dominant theoretical models		
	Classical PR	Professional PR	Corporate communication
Boundaries	Locus of control	Divergent	Convergent
Orientation	Greeks, Romans Pre-war USA	Post-war US/UK/Europe	Global
Ideology	Paternalistic	Collectivistic	Individualistic
Role	Public control	Systems management	Stakeholder relations
Relationship with main board	Administrative	Advisory/ executive	Strategic
Generic activity	Public affairs	Public relations	Divergent
Status of workforce	Staff	Employees	Professional class
Relations with media	Social	Legal	Psychological
Role of institutes/ unions	Marginal	Adversarial	Collaborative
Change	Slow	Moderate	Continuous
Market position	Protected	Stable	Competitive
Attitude	Social stability	Essential cost	Mutual/Co-dependence

Source: Oliver (2001)

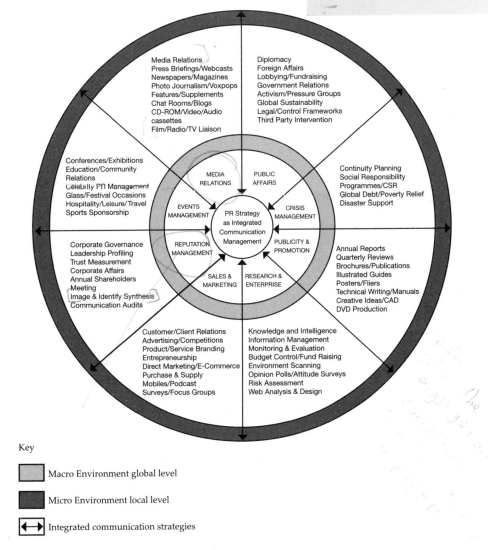

Key

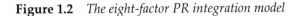

Macro Environment global level

Micro Environment local level

Integrated communication strategies

Source: Oliver (2008, 2006) A representation of the PR industry's eight key areas of academic specialisms and their associated professional clusters of activity.

Figure 1.2   *The eight-factor PR integration model*

- psychology;
- sociology;
- IT and computer studies;
- research methods;
- information studies including library/archival sourcing;
- journalism including technical writing;
- media studies including mass communication;
- advertising;
- marketing;
- business studies including transaction theory;
- management studies including change strategies;
- entrepreneurship;
- human resource management including organizational behaviour;
- civil and industrial law;
- ethics.

Universities still have difficulty in deciding whether to classify and invest in the study of this discipline as a 'media arts' subject area or a 'business and management' subject area. Media and creative arts faculty people approach public relations through journalism, film, radio and photography production (for events/publicity, etc) while business faculty people approach public relations through a management orientation based on planning and control in line with business strategy. Hands-on skills are learnt through workshops, sometimes provided by trainers/visitors, usually through the professional bodies such as the CIPR and IPRA, just as they are on continuous professional development (CPD) courses in accountancy, marketing or IT through their relevant bodies. However, the methodological principles for development of public relations as an academic discipline are based on accepted research methods, albeit depending on the purpose of a particular piece of research or analysis, as shown in Table 1.2.

Three main areas of popular academic research continue to be:

1. business and political communication strategy, which includes public or government affairs and corporate reputation;
2. governance and leadership communication strategy, involving employees, managers, directors and shareholders;
3. integrated marketing communication strategy.

As the three most research-based areas, they best support the public relations profession, both in Europe and the United States, at this stage in its history. The importance of the analytical approach for practitioners cannot be overestimated, given the critical role of monitoring and evaluation of campaign policy and planning in today's ever-changing multimedia, new technology context.

Semantics

A long-standing CIPR definition of public relations is 'the planned and sustained effort to establish and maintain goodwill and mutual understanding between an organization and its publics'. Here, the definition implies strategic management by the inclusion of the words 'planned' and 'sustained', and the use of the word 'publics' for stakeholders, interested parties and other influential groups. A more recent CIPR approach is to refer to public relations as being 'about reputation – the result of what you do, what you say and what others say about you', and 'the discipline which looks after reputation – with the aim of earning understanding and support, and influencing opinion and behaviour'.

Alternative practitioner definitions nearly always identify a strategic role for public relations when they are heard saying that public relations is the management of all communication within the organization and between the organization and its outside audiences. The purpose is to create better understanding of the organization among its audiences. Circumstances determine which audiences or sub-audiences are most important and need priority attention at any time.

Public relations practice involves management of an organization's reputation by identifying perceptions that are held of the organization and working to inform all relevant audiences about organizational performance. It is concerned with developing a deserved reputation for an organization, one that is based on solid performance not hollow hype. Reputation will not necessarily be favourable and may only be as favourable as the organization deserves. This becomes increasingly complex in the light of new technologies. Many CIPR members reject the notion of a change of name from 'public relations department' to 'corporate communication department' and argue that the impact of the internet on public relations is simply that it offers new electronic operational tools which don't alter essential practices. However, given that technology has so changed strategic operations for all forms of business and organizational communication, and given that human communication is the key measurable variable, the term 'corporate communication' better represents the theory and practice of this discipline in large organizations.

Underpinning these changes and developments is the convergence of traditional telecommunications industries. 'Time-to-market' for some communications technology firms often narrowed from 20 years to six months during the 1990s. This convergence has led to some of the most lucrative consultancy in the corporate communication profession as industry tried to cope with the rapid rate of change in company and commercial cultures. Thus we see that corporate communication is both divergent and convergent in theory and practice, requiring special, advanced multi-skilling and powers of strategic thinking and operational practice.

Table 1.2 *Key methods of data collection and methodological principles*

Method	Main purpose	Data collection	Sample	Analysis
Phenomenology Derived from philosophy	Study of the 'lived experience'	In-depth audiotaped interviews	Small purposive sample (usually between 6 and 20, though occasionally fewer), depending on the variety of experiences sampled	Exhaustive description; thematic analysis
Grounded theory Developed by sociologists to understand social issues	Generate theory from all available sources in a social setting	Semi-structured audiotaped interviews/focus groups, with or without observation/ documentary analysis	Usually between 20 and 40, but may be larger or smaller depending on the homogeneity of observations. Purposive sampling is followed by theoretical sampling until saturation of the data is achieved	Constant comparison – data analysis proceeds with data collection, sampling and development of the interview guide. Leads to emergent concepts and categories
Ethnography Developed within anthropology	Gain a perspective of a culture, for example an organizational setting	Participant observation including interviews with 'key informants'/ documentary sources, field notes/video recording	Focuses on fieldwork with 'immersion' in the setting. Numbers not relevant	Thick description – describes detailed pattern of social interactions and meanings

Narrative analysis/ life history Based on biographical studies	Detailed study of people's lives and experiences, based on the stories they tell	Audiotaped unstructured interviews that encourage story-telling. Often last up to 3 hours	Few participants (often 6 to 10), often interviewed on more than one occasion	Narrative analysis – focuses on thematic content, structure and coherence
Discourse analysis From linguistic studies	Study of the ways that social realities and understandings are constructed through language	Audiotaped or videotaped conversations, often in naturalistic settings	May be as small as 2, as in a professional–patient interaction	Detailed interpretive analysis of text, with a focus on the use of language and verbal expression
Conversation analysis From ethno-methodology	Detailed study of 'tacit' means of communication	Non-participant videotaped observations of everyday activities	May be as small as 2, as in professional–patient interaction	Detailed analysis of non-verbal and verbal interaction, including turn-taking
Case study Management studies	Non-participant investigation using a variety of qualitative and quantitative research methods to investigate a 'case'. The case may be an individual, a group of people with a common area of concern, or an organizational unit or setting			
Action research	Similar to a case study, but the researcher is usually an active participant within the setting and may act as a change agent. The focus of investigation is determined with the work-based team, findings shared, change negotiated, results evaluated, and further areas of investigation jointly determined			

Source: Adapted from Walker *et al* (2005)

While the public relations industry owes a debt of gratitude to the marketing industry for its development of numerous research tools and techniques, it has led to considerable semantic confusion. For example, one group of marketeers defined public relations as 'building good relations with the company's various publics by obtaining favourable publicity, building up a good corporate image and handling or heading off unfavourable rumours, stories and events' (Kotler *et al*, 1999). Such academic marketeers view public relations as a mass promotion technique and suggest that the old name for 'marketing public relations' was merely 'publicity', and 'seen simply as activities to promote a company or its products by planting news about it in media not paid for by the sponsor'.

Today, recognizing that public relations reaches beyond customers, the Chartered Institute of Marketing (CIM) concurs with the public relations industry that many marketing tactics such as media relations, press relations and product publicity are derived from the public relations industry. From a strategic point of view, this is important in terms of quality assurance. In global companies, a public relations or corporate communication department is never subjugated to the marketing department even though marketing strategy may be linked to corporate business strategy, because it fails to address the holistic links of strategic public relations with overall corporate strategy (see Figure 5.1 on page 104). Strategy is essentially longer-term planning while bottom line sales tactics, in spite of loyalty schemes, often demand short-term, if not immediate, results. Of course both can influence strategic decision making under changing circumstances.

Strategic public relations is concerned with managing the relationships between an organization and a much wider variety of stakeholders or audiences and range of priorities at any given time. The development of macroeconomics and environmental management studies has put pressure on the public relations industry to focus public relations strategy on the dimension of the enterprise or organization that goes beyond the bottom line of profit and shareholder price to include measures of corporate success based on social accountability. As well as an organization's role in the economic life of its country and its position in the global or national marketplace, public relations counsel and activities form an important part of an organization's policy in defining the environmental factors that affect its corporate business activities. These include social stratification, social welfare and national policy, technology, and the political, legal and regulatory processes appropriate to a particular organization or the industry in which it operates. All these factors need understanding of the attitudes and cultural norms that influence an organization's reputation and public acceptability.

Operational strategy

Public relations is practised in organizations ranging from SMEs to transnational, multinational corporations with budgets bigger than many countries' governments. Baskin *et al* (1997) say:

> Public relations practitioners communicate with all relevant internal and external publics to develop positive relationships and to create consistency between organizational goals and societal expectations. Public relations practitioners develop, execute and evaluate organizational programmes that promote the exchange of influence and understanding among an organization's constituent parts and publics.

Classic models of strategic management try to balance the internal and external perspectives by correlating corporate mission with external environmental factors over time. Adapting Pearce and Robinson (1982) cited in Grunig (1992), the public relations operations manager must:

- communicate the mission of the company, including broad statements;
- develop a company profile that reflects its internal condition and capability;
- assess the company's external environment, in terms of both competitive and general contextual factors;
- analyse possible options uncovered in the matching of the company profile with the external environment;
- identify desired options uncovered when the set of possibilities is considered in light of the company mission;
- communicate to all prioritized stakeholder groups the long-term objectives and grand strategies needed to achieve the desired options;
- develop annual objectives and short-term strategies that are compatible with the long-term objectives and grand strategies;
- implement strategic choice decisions using budgeted resources by matching tasks, people, structures, technologies and reward systems;
- review and evaluate the success or otherwise of strategic campaign processes to serve as a basis of control and as benchmarks for future decision making;
- incorporate ethical considerations into the decision-making cycle.

Inevitably, crucial factors in such an exercise are relations with the media and identifying the purpose, nature and nurture required of any desired communication, as indicated by Grunig and Hunt's summary in Table 1.3. Grunig (1992) identified half of US companies as using the public information model, 20 per cent using the two-way asymmetric model and only 15 per cent using one or other of the press agency/publicity model or the two-way symmetric model. Of course, no one model is mutually exclusive and all four models may be applied within a single programme, not necessarily simultaneously but as appropriate for specific requirements. Grunig and his researchers at the IABC asserted that quality assurance is best achieved through the two-way symmetrical model, which relies heavily on the analysis of feedback.

However, before looking at the role of feedback in best practice, it is necessary to revisit the concept of stakeholder theory and the responsibilities an organization carries in respect of its dealings with different groups, as shown in Table 1.4.

The role of public opinion in the behaviour of organizations continues to increase via the internet and, while the public relations profession has always been aware of its obligations to all stakeholder groups, a global economy is making for increasingly onerous relations. Edward Bernays said in 1923 that 'it is in the creation of a public conscience that the counsel on public relations is destined, I believe, to fulfil its highest usefulness to the society in which we live'. The CIPR today endorses this thinking, over 80 years later, in its code of conduct, as does the IPRA.

It has already been stated that communicating consistently between stakeholders or audiences does not mean communicating the same message. Rather, a fundamental requirement in public relations is to develop a consistent corporate message (and tone) that appropriately reflects the organization in the way that the organization wishes to be reflected, even as events, crises and issues are occurring. At the same time, messages must be capable of being adapted creatively to be understood by the different audiences targeted.

Ind (1997) wrote:

> Communication strategies should always start from the need to have specifically and ideally quantifiable communication objectives. The over-arching goal should be to achieve a specific positioning that will transcend the objectives for different audiences. The positioning itself should be derived from analysis.

Ind also suggests that public relations functions are to increase awareness and improve favourability:

> Public relations loses out to advertising in its controllability, but it has the advantage over advertising in its ability to communicate more complex messages and in its credibility. The press coverage achieved through media relations activity has the appearance of neutrality. Also the ability to target specific media and audiences is enhanced by the flexibility public relations offers. (p 80)

Table 1.3 *Four traditional public relations models*

Characteristic	*Model*			
	Press agency/ publicity	*Public information*	*Two-way asymmetric*	*Two-way symmetric*
Purpose	Propaganda	Dissemination of information	Scientific persuasion	Mutual understanding
Nature of communication	One-way; complete truth not essential	One-way; truth important	Two-way; imbalanced effects	Two-way; balanced effects
Communication model	Source → Receiver	Source → Receiver	Source ↔ Receiver ↔ Feedback	Group ↔ Group
Nature of research	Little; 'counting house'	Little; readability, readership	Formative; evaluation of attitudes	Formative; evaluation of understanding
Leading historical figures	P T Barnum	Ivy Lee	Edward L Bernays	Grunig *et al*, educators, professional leaders
Where practised today	Sports; theatre; product promotion; celebrity	Government; non-profit associations; business	Competitive business; PR agencies; consultancies	Regulated business; PR agencies; consultancies

Source: Adapted from Grunig and Hunt (1984)

This requires that a public relations strategy has to consider the ways that all its activities can be integrated, and the most practical and definitive way currently is to base public relations programmes on audience or stakeholder analysis. Just as it is critical to understand the theory and practice of customer relations in order to sell anything, so it is critical to understand what the different audiences or stakeholders need to know, where they are coming from in response to a message or organization's reputation, so that the principles of mutual understanding, not necessarily agreement, can be applied. As Ind says:

> a communication(s) strategy can then be evolved which specifies within an overall positioning the communication requirements for each specific audience. This should not encourage communication anarchy with messages

Table 1.4 *Stakeholders' responsibilities*

Stakeholders	Responsibilities	
1. Customers	Economic issues:	profitability competitive products survival of the company product quality
	Ethical issues:	honesty the best possible products and services satisfy customer needs
	Voluntary issues:	long-term business function development
2. Employees	Economic issues:	work and income
	Legal issues:	cooperation following the regulations in dismissal situations
	Ethical issues:	good working conditions stability and security developing possibilities honesty
	Voluntary issues:	education supporting activities and interests
3. Competitors	Ethical issues:	truthful information fair marketing and pricing practices no use of questionable practices consistency and stability playing the game by the rules
	Voluntary issues:	good relations cooperation in industry-related issues
4. Owners	Economic issues:	return on assets/investments securing investments maximizing cash flow solvency profits
	Ethical issues:	Adequate information

Stakeholders	Responsibilities	
5. Suppliers	Economic issues:	volumes profitability
	Ethical issues:	honesty
	Voluntary issues:	sustainable and reliable long-term relations
6. Community	Economic issues:	taxes employment
	Legal issues:	influence on trade balance
	Ethical issues:	following laws and regulations
	Voluntary issues:	behaving with integrity supporting local activities
7. Government	Economic issues:	taxes employment influence on trade balance
	Legal issues:	following laws and regulations
	Ethical issues:	behaving with integrity
	Voluntary issues:	supporting local activities
8. Financial groups	Economic issues:	profitability security of investment
	Ethical issues:	adequate information
9. The environment, eg pressure groups	Legal issues:	compliance with environmental regulations
	Ethical issues:	environmental friendliness protecting the environment product recycling
	Voluntary issues:	proactive environmental management
10. Old and new media, eg press, TV, web	Legal issues:	compliance with the law, eg invasion of privacy in celebrity PR
	General issues:	compliance with guidelines, codes of conduct and ethics statements
	Voluntary issues:	internal web pages and chat rooms

Source: Adapted from Aurila (1993), in Oliver (1997)

to shareholders contradicting those to consumers, but relevance. Working from audiences inwards encourages an organization to think of its communication mechanisms appropriately.

The feedback cycle

Given the close psychological connection between perception and communication, critical feedback data will include identifying the cyclical responses to a message from receivers over periods of time. The traditional emphasis on feedback as knowledge and intelligence is as important as ever, but is changing in scale as a result of computer software.

Webster's definition of 'feedback' is 'the return to the point of origin, evaluative or corrective action, about an action or a process'. What this means in operational public relations terms is that it is possible to provide computer-tabulated information for managers about a firm's stakeholder practices and behaviour. Because this information is based on day-to-day perceptions, it is a powerful tool for communication analysis, reflection and adjustment.

Feedback can be derived from two sources: those identified for a generic programme to help corporate communication managers focus on key behaviour of their audiences, and those identified on a custom basis where a number of activities or a particular group of stakeholders for the company are identified. Feedback questionnaires and reports usually cover two areas: frequency and importance. Frequency is the extent to which the corporate communication manager uses a particular activity as perceived by the group or behaviours being evaluated. Importance is the extent to which the corporate communication manager feels a particular activity, message or behaviour is important. A typical feedback report will cover a section-by-section summary giving specific scores for each activity and a listing of the 'top 10' activities in order of importance with scores for each.

Feedback provides three principal areas of application. First, it can be used in organizational surveys to determine the extent to which a company is following practices that reflect or help to change the organization's reputation or culture. Secondly, it can be used on a one-to-one counselling basis where the process provides bottom-up or lateral feedback to supplement the top-down view usually proposed in dealing with journalists and/or employees. Thirdly, it can be used as a basis for highly focused continuous professional training and development where managers are helped to improve their communication performance in areas where deficiencies are evidenced.

A typical research plan would always take into account both positive and negative feedback in its research brief, the work plan, data collection, analysis and evaluation. Given that stakeholder groups and subgroups may have cultural differences of language, religion, values and attitudes, aesthetics, education and social organization, feedback and the analytical tools applied to them are a specialist public relations activity.

Control vs co-dependency

Nowhere does the importance of feedback inform the public relations controller more than during a crisis, where the business continuity plan depends heavily on its quality control during and after a disaster. Taking control while being co-dependent during a crisis taxes the public relations skills of the most experienced practitioner. With the central command role of communication, he or she must manage the crisis centre overall in collaboration with other key personnel responsible for health and safety, HR, marketing and operations, as well as manage any number of media enquiries.

Luftman (2004) examined 245 companies with continuity plans and surveyed 350 business technology managers. Even allowing for multiple responses, he showed the significance of the PR role during a crisis, which I later developed in my action stations framework. The Luftman data, shown in Figure 1.3, was published in *Information Week,* with the public relations roles emphasized to include human resources, because there would usually be much internal public relations activity during a crisis.

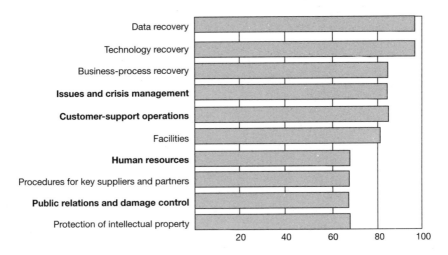

Source: Luftman (2004)

Figure 1.3   *Communication and the business continuity plan (BCP)*

CAMPAIGN: NESTLÉ

The campaign came about following research by Nestlé into the problems faced by young people. With a dwindling number of youth clubs, there were insufficient places for young people to go after school. Further research showed that after-school activities were funded at an average 17p per day per young person – limiting local authorities' ability to offer activity and support to teenagers. 'Make Space' was created in 2002 by the leading children's charity, 4Children, in conjunction with its long-time supporter Nestlé UK, for which adding value to the societies in which it operates is one of its core worldwide strategies.

Challenge vs opportunity

The Make Space campaign set out in 2007 to create a model for contemporary 'places to go' for young people, to promote this model – often via local authorities, which administer the majority of clubs – and to lobby for more funding and support from the British government whose Comprehensive Spending Review was imminent.

'Youth Matters', a Green Paper published in 2005 for consultation by the government, focused on 'opportunity cards' and while these undoubtedly would have potential, Make Space did not believe that they offered a long-term solution to the problem of where young people could go after school.

Research

Nestlé's 2002 research was updated via a road show visiting nine centres, which explored 16,000 young people's thoughts and attitudes via consultations and focus groups in schools, youth clubs and groups.

The efficacy of the Make Space model of integrated provision was independently evaluated by the Institute of Education in a six-month study using a selection of clubs and centres.

A survey of the awareness and attitudes towards Make Space and youth provision was carried out amongst parliamentarians and a range of opinion leaders within the youth sector in order to inform communication planning/key messages.

Strategic plan

- Highlight the limitations of proposed policy.
- Show that Make Space represented a significant constituency – 1,300 clubs representing nearly 300,000 young people at the start of 2007.
- Show that the Make Space model of integrated provision created better outcomes for young people.
- Listen to young people and make their voices heard in the call for change.
- Create a campaign momentum culminating in high-profile interest to demand attention.

The campaign would be judged by its ability to generate substantial new funding from central government to develop youth centres through the country and to support other measures called for by young people (as determined by the research amongst the 16,000 mentioned above) and voiced by the Make Space Youth Review.

Core targets were The Treasury, the DfES; young people of secondary school age (11–16); local authorities, in particular youth services personnel; and the general public (as a means of demonstrating that the issue was of wide public interest). The key messages to be conveyed were:

- Investment in Britain's young people was required urgently.
- Boredom leads to anti-social behaviour.
- Youth centres (adopting the Make Space integrated model) were a solution called for by young people.

The strategy was to engage with government whilst lobbying for desired outcomes via:

- creating a Youth Review (expect members comprising academics, politicians, youth services specialists and young people) to evaluate the current youth offer and make recommendations;
- feeding in the findings of the youth consultation (road show) to the Review;
- engaging with and working in tandem with the government's own Treasury/DfES review;
- engaging with the Treasury via frequent meetings, interchanging ideas and findings, and by ensuring that the road show visited the constituencies of every Treasury minister;
- creating an impactful media campaign around the launch of the Youth Review findings and recommendations.

The campaign was guided by a working group chaired by the Make Space Manager with support from his team and Nestlé specialists, whose expertise was invaluable in complementing that of the charity.

Operational strategy

Late 2006/quarter one 2007: the Make Space Youth Review, under political campaigner Oona King, undertook a comprehensive consultation with 16,000 young people via a road show.

Quarter two 2007: an interim report was published, backed up by a mass youth lobby of parliament and the findings were presented to Gordon Brown at Number 11 by young people. The lobby, in which young people were dressed as 'hoodies' with the slogan 'Tell Us Where to Go' was extensively covered across national media. The night before, as part of a striking 24-hour press trailer, an image of a 'hoodie' with the message 'Look Behind the Hoodie' was projected onto London landmarks including Marble Arch and the Houses of Parliament.

The decision to produce an interim report was taken as a precaution, in case the government completed its own deliberations before the Make Space final report was complete. The report was mailed to a list of over 1,000 opinion formers to create public support for the findings and recommendations of the Youth Review before the government began to finalize its own recommendations.

Quarter three: a second publicity drive was staged featuring youth icon Lily Allen – she had been approached by the campaign team on the basis of her previous pronouncements on the need for more support for young people and her obvious appeal to youth and the media. The Make Space entourage led by Ms Allen was invited to Number 10 and the Prime Minister received the final report. Extensive media coverage followed.

Subsequently, Make Space received a request from the Prime Minister to attend another meeting in Number 10, involving three of his Cabinet to discuss the findings and recommendations of the Make Space report and, in response, to launch a government 10-year Youth Strategy. An hour-long meeting took place in the Cabinet Room with young people in Make Space T-shirts. Gordon Brown stayed for 45 minutes and the proceedings were covered in national and specialist media.

Following the publicity, members of the Make Space Youth Cabinet were filmed assessing the new strategy with the Children's Commissioner, for BBC TV.

Campaign outcomes

The 220 media reports comprised:

- 16 national newspaper reports;
- 86 regional newspaper reports;
- 22 trade magazine reports;
- 56 World Wide Web reports;
- 40 broadcast reports.

One or more key messages were included in 74 per cent of media reports.

The Make Space lobby resulted in the announcement within the government's Youth Strategy of £100 million new investment in youth services, 70 per cent to be spent on youth clubs.

Several other Make Space recommendations were incorporated in the Strategy, including the pledge that 25 per cent of the spending of new funds would be decided by young people.

REFLECTION

Based on the information provided:

1. With reference to the broad theories of relationships described in the chapter, what type or types of relationship did Nestlé develop with its key stakeholder groups?
2. What factors influenced the campaign strategy?
3. How might the local decision outcomes impact on the company's global reputation?
4. By applying the eight-factor PR integration model, identify which technical activities contributed to the success of the campaign and thus which of the eight strategic areas took precedence.
5. Using the BCP plan, suggest how the nature and quality of feedback will support the organization in the longer term.

2

PR'S PLACE ON THE BOARD:
A core governance role

Only 3 per cent of communication directors are thought to be currently on the main boards of UK companies and 23 per cent are on executive committees of FTSE-100 companies, according to research compiled by global public relations firm, Echo Research. However, the complexity of life in the 21st century is bringing public relations expertise back to the table, with a place on the main board in a joint governance role. After a decade or so of global criticism, industry and commerce are alert to the needs for joint steering. The public relations director is unlikely to be the CEO's favourite colleague and he or she may frequently want to 'kill the messenger', but a competent CEO will trust both positive and negative counsel, so that advice is respected and appropriately rewarded.

Organizations deal with pressures and developments from both internal and external drivers, usually concurrently, but previously it was often only in times of crisis that an organization valued public relations input. Most corporate decision making distinguishes between objective and subjective interpretation of events, takes a continuous view of change rather than reacting immediately to turbulent or sudden change, and approaches corporate strategy as a process involving choices rather than determinate positions. Managing public relations strategic decision making is no different and, like accounting or law, public relations has its own body of knowledge, rules and regulations. However, it requires commitment from the CEO and main board members if the public relations director is to be able to fulfil his or her remit by applying such knowledge with the authority required.

Public relations advice has traditionally relied on case studies and empirical research to provide a base on which to draw and develop models of theory and best practice. Few practitioner writers adopt a polemical position about the communication aspects of public relations; yet, like most fledgling academic disciplines or professions, they are often criticized for being too descriptive and banal. An upsurge in the number of public relations research consultancies and an increase in client billings are an indication of recognition of the need for proven expertise at strategic level.

Costing communication

The CEO will want to extract value for money and insist on measured justification for public relations expenditure, but a strong, transformational leader will recognize the dangers inherent in not having expert public relations communication input at board meetings. Canadian writer Gareth Morgan (1997) looked at management performance and there is not one of his nine leadership competence modes in which communication does not play a central operational role; see Table 2.1.

It has been reported that on average CEOs spend between 50 and 80 per cent of their working hours on communicating with stakeholders of one sort or another, which suggests that they not only develop strategy but must be seen to operationalize it through the key competency of communication

Table 2.1 *Communication in leadership*

Cultural model	*Communication/PR model*
• Reading the environment • Proactive management • Leadership and vision • Human resource management • Promoting creativity, learning and information • Skills of remote management • Using information technology • Managing complexity • Developing contextual competencies	• Environmental scanning (external forces), issues, management, planning, monitoring and evaluation • Mission/intelligence data • Relationship building/perception • Adaptive/interpretive strategies • Media relations, lobbying • Interdisciplinary nature of PR/crisis management • A management discipline involving a wide variety of stakeholder relations

Source: Oliver (2001), based on Morgan (1997)

Table 2.2 *Importance of global leadership compared with other needs (based on a survey of US* Fortune 500 *Firms)*

Dimension	Average rating
Competent global leaders	6.1
Adequate financial resources	5.9
Improved international communication technology	5.1
Higher quality local national workforce	5.0
Greater political stability in developing countries	4.7
Greater national government support of trade	4.5
Lower tariff/trade restrictions in other countries	4.4

(1 = Not at all important; 7 = Extremely important)
Source: Gregerson *et al* (1999)

and concomitant public relations, although it is rarely identified; see the first mention in Table 2.2.

A recent example illustrating this point is the case of Sir Fred Goodwin who was a celebrity in the banking industry in Britain, who fell from grace to become what the media called 'the world's worst banker'. His bank lost £28 billion and is now under state control. The British government Treasury select committee, who met with Sir Fred, heard from other representatives of the investment industry of the problems in the global financial system that have been caused by a critical failure of leadership and corporate governance – not the 'masters of the universe' portrayed by Tom Wolfe in his *Bonfire of the Vanities*. Whether or not these institutions paid any attention to the internal public relations practitioner's advice to be more attentive to shareholder concerns, to communicate and act upon those concerns is a moot point. Peter Chambers, head of the investment arm of Legal & General, said at the hearing that 'their campaign to curb the power and modify the strategy of Sir Fred Goodwin at Royal Bank of Scotland came to nothing until it was far too late'. As columnist Anthony Hilton wrote, 'it is precisely when times are difficult as they are currently and the system is severely stretched that rules... and corporate governance come into their own'.

Perhaps the tools of the internet will help Peter Chambers' mission. Some institutional websites, however, set up and run by in-house public relations departments, only run the good news stories or ones that they want circulated asymmetrically or virally. The leaders of today are going to have to join the blogging revolution to be seen to engage with shareholders, civil servants, media and customers alike, symmetrically. The current generation of young qualified PR practitioners who are au fait with platforms such as Twitter are entering a new era of sophisticated, honest and meaningful public relations.

The public relations specialist will investigate and analyse internal and external pressures, diagnose problems confronting the organization, suggest future trends and developments, and propose or counsel prescriptions for future action and, in the case of crisis management, remedial action; together, these activities are generally referred to as 'environmental scanning'. To analyse the pressures and problems confronting the employing organization or company, it is understood that a number of proactive public relations processes are needed. These include using a variety of methods for collating public relations data such as:

- electronic sources such as CD-ROM library indexes and other organizational sources and external reference materials;
- different interpretations of the public relations problem that incorporate perceptions of target audiences, including the media;
- the extent to which it is possible to define and predict future trends;
- the contribution of managers and employees as a resource in meeting the public relations campaign or corporate communication objectives.

Van Riel's model shown in Figure 2.1 gives the strategic public relations director a focus for choosing a particular type of communication policy, by analysing the firm's corporate strategy in relation to the similarity or otherwise of the driving forces affecting the firm's mission, the amount or nature of control exercised by the board directors and the scale of environmental pressure on the organization. The communication policy is then derived from measures of endorsement, uniformity and variety.

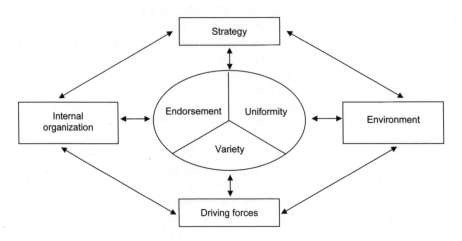

Source: van Riel (1995)

Figure 2.1   *Factors in the choice of communication policy*

One of the criticisms of the corporate strategy literature is that it rarely makes a distinction between different organizations in terms of their ownership, organizational size and mission. Clearly, private companies, voluntary bodies and public services adopt different approaches to their organization and objectives, but this is reflected more in the culture of each organization rather than in the process of communication. The fundamental nature of human communication may be universal but message style and delivery may change to best fit the culture in which it is being set.

From function to strategy

To illustrate this point, perhaps one of the most helpful strategic management models for communication purposes is the Johnson and Scholes (2002) model adapted here in Figure 2.2.

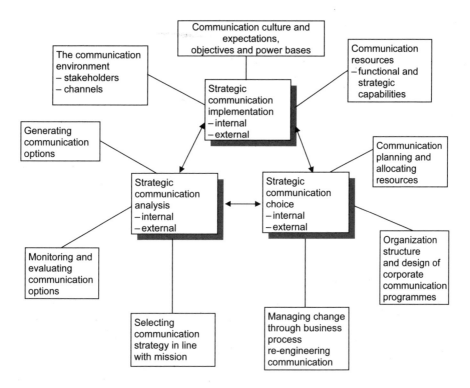

Source: Oliver (1997), adapted from Johnson and Scholes (1993)

Figure 2.2 *Aligning communication leadership to corporate strategy*

There are a number of weaknesses in this model, or at least potential for misunderstanding. While the model shows the essential elements of the strategy process, it is not linear, starting at the establishment of a mission and ending with implementation. As all competent public relations practitioners know, these processes must run in parallel and with consideration of resources and the practicalities of implementation. Johnson and Scholes attempt to discuss the process of managing strategically through human resources and make the reader more aware of the tactical requirements necessary for the strategy process to be effective. They include a model of stakeholder mapping to characterize stakeholders in terms of their level of power and interest in any outcome. They offer the model shown in Figure 2.3 as a useful analytical tool in assessing communication priorities at any given time.

		Level of interest	
		Low	High
Power	Low	Minimal effort	Keep informed
	High	Keep satisfied	Keep players

Source: Johnson and Scholes (2002)

Figure 2.3   *Stakeholder mapping matrix*

This approach suggests that, although mission statements articulate organizational objectives and these objectives are usually derived from economic managerial or social responsibility considerations, stakeholders have expectations that may not always be met. These expectations relate to the performance of the organization as well as being influenced by the external cultural context in which the organization is operating. Stakeholders have different degrees of power to determine the objectives of an organization and various levels of interest in exercising that power, and so stakeholder objectives affect the development of future organizational strategies.

Business re-engineering in the 1980s challenged firms to think more deeply about process. The systems approach to management is not just a process of analysis and reductionism but one of linking things together – the process of synthesis. In the 1990s, Johnson and Scholes produced a model for analysing organizational culture which, they argued, was essential if synthesis were to occur. They referred to the interplay of various factors in organizational culture as the cultural web or the mindset of an organization – that is to say, the way it sees itself and its environment. In Figure 2.4, they suggest formal and informal ways that organizational systems work through important relationships (structure); core groupings (power); measurement and reward systems (control); behavioural norms (stories); training (rituals); language and livery (symbols); and process and expected competencies (routine). There can only be synthesis if communication is performed to a high standard in linking together these strategic areas for competitive advantage.

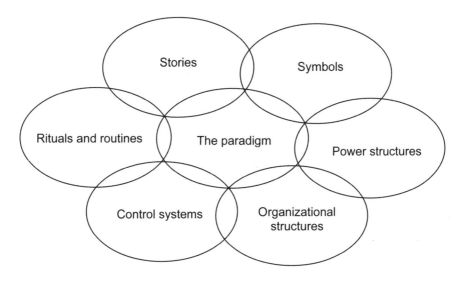

Source: Johnson and Scholes (2002)

Figure 2.4   *The cultural web*

On a more philosophical note, it is worth considering here how these factors make up a paradigm, as the organizational paradigm lies at the heart of any public relations strategy. It describes a set of preconceptions that underlie people's way of looking at the world in general, not just an organization. It comprises a set of assumptions that people rarely question. From time to time a paradigm is shaken up and a paradigm shift takes place. In such an event, textbooks have to be rewritten as it involves the rethinking of basic assumptions underlying people's perceptions. Paradigm shifts, that is, fundamental changes in the ruling paradigm, are rarely dramatic in business and management, although electronic communications and global technology are accelerating change pertaining to the ruling paradigm of strategic public relations theory and practice.

Electronic systems and processes, particularly in respect of media relations, are working on an underlying set of assumptions and beliefs that are changing and undergoing a revolutionary paradigm shift as a result of the cultural implications of globalization. At such times, organizations impose tighter controls. For instance, there are few organizations where managers are allowed to differ openly from or criticize the official line on strategy and policy, yet this may lie at the heart of the public relations expert counsel. Adherence to the accepted way of running an organization and the markets within which an organization is operating may not be openly criticized, and internal communication will attempt to reflect and reinforce the official line, through the company newsletter, for example.

Cognitive dissonance: coping with conflict

Stacey's (1991) approach to strategy takes conflicts inherent in any organizational processes resting on cultural differences and change, and provides a model of *ordinary* and *extraordinary* management. Modern models of strategy formulation stress the instability of the relationship between an organization and its environment because time and dynamics never stand still. In any organization there is a perceived need to maintain stability and harmony while making sure that the organization can change in order to survive. This contradiction is expressed by Stacey as ordinary management on the one hand and extraordinary management on the other. These are useful concepts to critically appraise the role of public relations in corporate strategy. They reflect the fundamental philosophy of public relations in that the overall corporate message must be consistent (ordinary management) while monitoring changes in stakeholder perceptions that could impact on corporate objectives (extraordinary management) and which in turn lead to changes in the message.

The challenge for strategic public relations is to accept widely that, for efficient operation at any given time, it is necessary for an organization to have a clear sense of purpose and unity, but also a parallel culture in which it is possible to raise safely a variety of viewpoints to challenge complacency and ensure survival. Clinical psychology tells us that it is important that cognitive feedback loops operate in a positive manner so that perception and communication can be updated and clarified where appropriate. This is the basis of the symmetrical models promoted by Grunig (1992).

Public relations choices are made on the basis of rational criteria, but this is only possible when there is agreement on what the business is all about and what kind of environment it has to cope with. Stacey argues that managers only operate within bounded rationality. The complexities of modern organizations mean that they have to adopt a pragmatic approach to decision making and accept that they cannot conceptualize or accommodate all possibilities. Bureaucratic procedures help to simplify the manager's task, providing rules and procedures for tackling many decisions. A hierarchical management structure ensures that difficult decisions can be made within the context of the prevailing ideology – the official line of the ruling coalition.

Ordinary PR management

Ordinary management is necessary to ensure that targets can be met and that the organization survives through rational processes. It presupposes a stable environment and can only be practised in contained change situations. It is not a negative concept given that it must be practised if an organization is to be able to control and deliver competitive advantage. It also implies that public relations, however, is conducted on the basis of asymmetrical communication in which the organization 'gets what it wants without changing its behaviour or without compromising' (Grunig and White, 1992).

The asymmetric nature of public relations means that the organization will find it difficult to adapt to a changing environment because it does not recognize that communication with the outside, as well as with its own employees, must be a two-way process. Stacey's (1993: 72) definition of extraordinary management states that it is 'the use of intuitive, political, group learning modes of decision-making and self-organizing forms of control in open-ended change situations. It is the form of management that managers must use if they are to change strategic direction and innovate'.

Extraordinary PR management

Despite the potential dangers for organizations remaining exclusively dedicated to ordinary management, a closer look at what is involved in extraordinary management will explain British reticence. Extraordinary management involves questioning and shattering paradigms and then creating new ones. It is a process that depends critically on contradiction and tension. The changing of paradigms is a revolutionary rather than an evolutionary process and cannot be intended by the organization. Stacey argues that both forms of management have to coexist if the organization is to evolve and survive a changing environment. An organization needs to provide a stable basis for meeting its short-term objectives and targets while at the same time providing a basis for transforming itself in the future to respond to changes in the environment.

Some organizations fail to recognize the need to allow for extraordinary management and instead rely on radical changes of CEOs, chief executives, consultants and other outside change agents who have little understanding of the nature of the problems within the organization. This is where the public relations consultant has to be particularly aware and cautious of the conflicting demands that may be put upon service provision. Many practitioners argue that they do what they're asked, no more no less, within the brief and the fee. In that they are professionally pragmatic. However, that approach may not be conducive to being consciously aware of where a particular service provision fits into the overall scheme of things. When monitoring and evaluating the wider environment, important elements are dependent on perception of how change in one area can impact on other areas or overall.

The implications of ordinary management for public relations are familiar through relationships with major stakeholders:

- *Shareholders* – the annual report is a regular calendar project. For most shareholders asymmetrical communication of results will tend to apply, whereas with major institutional shareholders self-interest will dictate a degree of symmetrical communication, and a genuine desire to listen to their concerns will be essential and generally implemented.
- *Customers* – the marketing and sales departments will tend to dominate in this aspect of the public relations role but, increasingly, symmetrical communication is being recognized as essential to obtain competitive advantage through 'relationship marketing'. A long-term two-way relationship may be established with customers to allow for feedback into marketing strategy. Grant and Schlesinger (1995) developed the concept of 'value exchange' in which a company optimizes the relationship between the financial investment a company makes in particular customer relationships and the return that customers generate by the specific way they choose to respond to the company's offering. For this, careful attention to the behaviour of customers is essential.
- *Employees* – the ruling coalition within the organization can of course use a wide range of channels to communicate with employees to achieve the aim or harmony, fit or convergence to a particular configuration and to ensure that they share the same mental models or paradigms. Posters that repeat the published mission statement, memos, messages contained in the actions of management relating to discipline suggestions and so on all contribute to an overall strategic process.

Implications of ordinary and extraordinary management

The implications of extraordinary management for public relations are significant. The need for extraordinary management in order for the organization to survive and flourish in an unstable environment has been emphasized, but control of the extraordinary process has to be achieved by informal organization of its activities. As the formal organization exists to protect the paradigm, the status quo, managers who wish to change the paradigm have to operate within an informal organization in informal groups that they organize themselves. These groups can cope with uncertainty and ambiguity – anathema to the formal bureaucracy – and tap into each other's perceptions of what is going on in the organization. According to Stacey, these groups are essentially political in nature. People handle conflicting interests through persuasion and negotiation, implicit bargaining of one person's contribution or interests for another's, and power exerted by means of influence rather than authority. This informal system has been referred to as 'the network system' and often lies at the heart of public relations expertise. It can coexist with hierarchy and bureaucracy, but must be encouraged by the actions of the bureaucracy and supported by top management.

When organizations manage successfully to combine ordinary with extraordinary management to create an innovative culture while maintaining stability, a sound public relations strategy plays a core role in sustaining the firm's corporate strategy. Both support competitive advantage while ensuring the capability to ward off hostile competition, pressure groups and the media.

Extraordinary management may lead to groups within the organization attempting to undermine the control of the organization and, ultimately, the ability of the organization to adapt requires that subversive activity takes place without control being lost. Decisions are not made by organizations as such, but rather by dominant coalitions within organizations, and these coalitions are not likely to be defined clearly in the official organization chart. White and Dozier (1992) argue that dominant coalitions still need information to help them make decisions. This is frequently provided by 'boundary spanners' – individuals within the organization who frequently interact with the organization's environment and relay information to the dominant coalition.

The CEO as cultural icon

The strategic challenge for most organizations today is adapting their structures, processes and cultures to achieve sound relationships built on long-term mutual advantage through the integration of internal and external communication. The principles and communication processes of public relations contribute to all cultural aspects of an organization, with the CEO as the figurehead or cultural icon, becoming a representative and leader of the organization's culture by his or her management style. Grunig *et al* were really discussing management style when they advocated symmetrical communication as best practice and, in today's language, the management style can often drive the corporate brand. As Ind (1997: 13) writes:

> A corporate brand is more than just the outward manifestation of an organization, its name, logo, visual presentation. Rather it is the core of values that defines it... Communications must be based on substance. If they are not, inconsistency creeps in and confusion follows shortly thereafter... What defines the corporation in comparison with the brand is the degree of complexity. It is larger, more diverse and has several audiences that it must interact with. The corporate brand must be able to meet the needs of the often competing claims of its stakeholders. To achieve that it must have clarity of vision, of values and of leadership.

The critical role of communication in operationalizing corporate mission and translating it into reality, and the importance of vision in the achievement of corporate objectives, are based on perception as a measurable variable of reality. Strategic planning models relate to public relations planning through open systems theory and general management tools such as hard line (not necessarily bottom line) value-added concepts. Many public relations professionals will argue that this is not new. Such factors have always existed as benchmarks for justifying their intangible but critical contribution. The difference today is that IT capability produces a variety of identifiable factors that can be seen to be part of an organization's intellectual capital, if not essential to its survival on occasions.

The public relations expert acts as specialist counsel to a corporate boardroom and his or her technical input is fundamental to management in sourcing, analysing, assessing, managing and tracking information and translating that information for the benefit of the corporate whole. Through flexibility and change, organizations today have to be lifelong learning organizations. They must encourage effective symmetrical communication to such an extent that external audiences such as the media and dominant political coalitions can occasionally influence or even drive strategy from time to time without destabilizing it. An organization making policy in response to public criticism alone may prove to have revealed weak management based on poor strategic planning.

Performance assessment

Public relations strategy, like any other variable in corporate planning, must be able to identify measurable performance indicators. The eight-factor assessment shown in Figure 2.5 is a checklist, with each variable having its own tools and techniques in the short- and longer-term operating schedules.

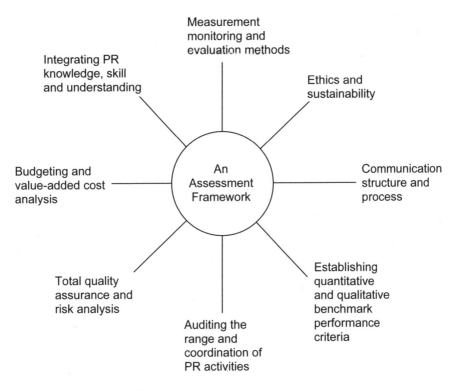

Source: Oliver (1997, 2004)

Figure 2.5 *PR performance indicators*

In monitoring and measuring performance, in-house or consultant public relations professionals act as boundary spanners by translating meaning from and about the organization in relation to the environment. They will counsel the CEO and top management about the organization's implicit assumptions. White and Dozier (1992) describe the case of a logging company, which might view trees as a crop to be harvested rather than a natural resource to be cherished. Indeed, the logging company's traditional world view is embedded in its language as, for example, when it refers to 'timber strands', a term implying that trees are there to be harvested like 'strands' of corn. During a symmetrical communication process, conflict between an organization and environmental pressure groups can be forestalled if public relations professionals fulfil their role as boundary spanners by ensuring that there is a two-way exchange of information or perception between the organization, the groups involved and the wider, often media-led environment.

In another example, from local government, the dominant and ruling left-wing coalition within a UK local authority might have a world view that saw the town for which they are responsible as consisting of needy people with rights to subsidy and support. A different, say right-wing, group might view the situation as one consisting of local council taxpayers being burdened with payments and challenge money going to needy people who may be exempt from paying council tax. In this latter case, the public relations task would be to increase awareness and modify the unidimensional view of the dominant coalition while simultaneously communicating the needs of the poor to the ratepayers within the community without loss of coherence.

Communicating risk

As operational risks increase faster than organizations learn to manage them effectively, many companies still perceive risk management as a cost instead of an investment. Randy Nornes, Executive Vice President of Aon Global Americas, said that 'resilient companies view risk management as an investment in future success'. So he defines enterprise resiliency as 'the ability to understand, avoid and adapt to disruptions while finding new opportunities for growth'. In the 2007 risk research, Aon listed 10 key risks in which 48 per cent of the sample mentioned the importance of being prepared for damage to reputation and 41 per cent of those surveyed referred to regulatory and legislative changes such as compliance with laws, regulations, contracts, policies, clear disclosure, solvency and community reinvestment.

John Kay, a leading British financial journalist and economist, when writing about the 2008/09 banking crisis argued that there had been an 'over-reliance on risk models based on inherently unknowable future events'. He believes that we:

> deal with uncertainties through stories rather than probabilities. Thinking about probabilities does not come easily to the human mind. Constructing narratives does. We weave stories and fit events and expectations into them. Our ability to tell stories is a valuable asset, the means by which we make sense of disconnected information.

In attempting to predict and manage the risk inherent in government regulation and legislation, lobbying has become big business. Although the public relations strategist will make sense of disconnected information through sound communication and the construction of narrative, the lobbyist attempts to influence government about issues that are relevant or threatening to the business. This type of political action, often called 'public affairs' instead of 'public relations', aims to exert explicit pressure on government decision makers.

There are different types of lobbying such as atmosphere setting or awareness raising processes; monitoring regulation through political relationships by providing information to policy makers; and through consultancy whereby politicians can be provided with knowledge on specific industrial and civic matters, perhaps through trade and professional associations or charities. Clearly there are situations in which this is a valuable democratic process, but questions have been raised in the recent past about influence turning to pressure turning to advocacy, thereby questioning levels of legitimacy. In the British government there is a Code of Conduct that prevents members of the House of Lords amending laws on behalf of lobbyists or businesses that are paying them. The rules on advocacy are the same for the House of Commons and Members of Parliament can be expelled if they accept financial inducement as an incentive or reward for exercising parliamentary influence or promoting any matter in return for payment or any other material benefit.

The problem for the PR practitioner is where to draw the line between offering expertise and the buying of political influence. Most large companies will have a government relations specialist who, through best communication practice will regularly scrutinize the external relations between their organization and government stakeholders. Although success in getting a law changed or not is often reported in financial terms, there may well be benefits to an organization's image and reputation requiring acute political judgement on the lobbyist's part.

It is pertinent to mention here the significance of language in attempting to influence politicians. The economics academic G R Steel stated in a recent letter to a British national newspaper that 'the meltdown in financial markets occurred, not because of insights or lack of insights... but because "uncertainties" were treated as "risks". And upon that error, "foolproof" algorithms for hedging financial bets delivered fools' gold'. John Kay says 'financial risk models are only as good as the correspondence between the model and the world'. The lobbyist is the correspondent. Clearly with sustainability at the forefront of the global agenda, issues of business growth tax the minds of all parties. This means that business has a higher political role to play with government than ever before, with government itself influencing, albeit imposing sustainable business and commercial practice. While businesses may be concerned with short-term profits, government must look to future generations. In the advanced economies, regulatory activity for sustainability is often carried out by voluntary agreement, but the role of government will often be to enforce the rules for the benefit of the wider society. Throughout the relationship between lobbyist and politician, it pays to remember the rule of symmetrical communication to ensure that what is said is what is heard and interpreted correctly.

The public relations search for strategic factors in the environment cannot ignore the future, however difficult it is to assess. There are innumerable cases of organizations that failed to spot the changes looming ahead which either threatened them or which provided opportunities for development that were then lost to competitors.

McMaster (1996) said that the past is a poor basis for predicting the future, an aim which is in any case not attainable. What organizations can do is to see their future by examining the structure and process of the present. McMaster is stressing that, although it is impossible to predict future detail, the structure of any future is a set of relationships within a complex system that is constantly adapting. For example, relationships with technology and other forces are always affecting the environment within which the organization operates. The challenge of foresight is the 'vast space of possibility' and McMaster cites 3M's success in organizing for foresight. New products form a very high percentage of its product range at any one time. These products have arisen not only from individual acts of foresight but from an organizational design and management culture that continually encourages new product ideas. In other words, the organization is itself the source of invention.

Nevertheless, the starting point for the development of future strategy usually involves a systematic analysis of the organization's environment from a review of external factors. Popular models are based on PESTLE, the interaction between factors in politics, economics, society, technology, law and environment/ecology. Such models are beginning to appear static, with a tendency to drive out more positive visions of what the future might hold for a particular organization, when people start to think creatively 'outside the box' through the drive and ambition of a transformational leader.

The word 'transparency' has become a cliché when debating the credibility of financial reporting, but it is now expected that all financial reporting should be transparent, timely, reliable and comparable. A European Directive requires both individual organizations and groups of companies to incorporate a 'fair review' in their annual reports; see Figure 2.6.

Inevitably, any vision of the future depends on resources. The strategic importance of a focus on resources arises because, ultimately, profits can be seen as a return on the resources controlled and owned by the firm. However, resources are divided into tangible and intangible resources. For each of these, there are usually key indicators, or a way of measuring their value. Public relations practitioners have often been caught in a mire of

---

The consolidated annual report shall include at least a fair review of the development and performance of the business and of the position of the undertakings included in the consolidation taken as a whole, together with a description of the principal risks and uncertainties that they face.

The review shall be a balanced and comprehensive analysis of the development and performance of the business and of the position of the undertakings included in the consolidation taken as a whole, consistent with the size and complexity of the business. To the extent necessary for an understanding of such development, performance or position, the analysis shall include both financial and, where appropriate, non-financial key performance indicators relevant to the particular business, including information relating to environmental and employee matters.

In providing its analysis, the consolidated annual report shall, where appropriate, provide references to and additional explanations of amounts reported in the consolidated accounts.

Where a consolidated annual report is required in addition to an annual report, the two reports may be presented as a single report. In preparing such a single report, it may be appropriate to give greater emphasis to those matters which are significant to the undertakings included in the consolidation taken as a whole.

Source: 2003/51/EC Article 2, paragraph 10

Figure 2.6   *Communicating the annual report*

confusion in an attempt at offering hard measures for intangible outcomes. Intangible resources, which used not to appear on UK balance sheets, are difficult to value objectively, even when recognized as being of value, but the UK now supports the public relations industry with statutory regulations that address this key element of worth.

Reputation vs the operating and financial review

The mandatory reporting of non-financial performance for large companies is an important development in the publication of annual reports and accounts and therefore reputation.

Non-financial performance was largely perceived as an additional public relations exercise, but narrative reports on intangible assets as core communication factors are now recognized as important to tangible outcomes. The CIPR framework shown in Figure 2.7 offers a practical five-stage plan for preparing an operating and financial review (OFR) for the annual report.

The value of a recognized brand name that is held in good esteem may be unrecoverable once lost. Sometimes value can be inferred when an acquisition takes place, the difference between the book valuation and the purchase price being denoted as goodwill arising on acquisition.

The CIPR definition of public relations as the planned and sustained effort to establish and 'maintain goodwill' and mutual understanding between an organization and its publics is, though, rarely enough. Goodwill needs to be grounded and made concrete. It has to be measured and accounted

Stage 1	Stage 2	Stage 3	Stage 4	Stage 5
Task Force	Stakeholder Audit	Benchmarking	Reporting Methods	Success Measurement

Stage 1

Board
Duty of the directors of qualifying companies is to produce an OFR: future plans, opportunities, risks and strategies

Key role for non-executive directors

Establish a Task Force to drive the OFR initiative

Task Force
Composition, corporate communications and other functional heads, non-executive directors, others who interface with stakeholders

Workshop to gain buy-in of Task Force members and key contribution

OFR Content and Process
Plan of OFR programme and responsibilities

Corporate success model (objectives, strategies, values etc) as benchmark

Stage 2

Task Force
Evaluation of stakeholder communication needs – internal and external including non-shareholders.

Prioritize audiences:

Primary	Secondary
Shareholders	Analysts
Investors	Media
Employees	Consumer organizations
Suppliers	Government/ NGOs
Distributors	Regulators
Consumers	Trade unions
Communities	Potential customers
Pressure groups	

Stakeholder Audit – scope:
Research (existing/ commissioned)
Focus groups/questionnaires
Anecdotal Information
Findings and 'gaps'
Key issues
Risk assessment
Reconcile stakeholder differences

Results
Better understanding of how the company is perceived:
Awareness and perceptions
Reputation drivers
Relationships
Strengths and weaknesses
Communication effectiveness: messages & methods versus OFR criteria
Analysis
Action plan

Stage 3

Task Force
(plus optional external auditor) Comparison of reporting practice with OFR criteria, with peer companies and against the company's own success model

Performance against OFR criteria

Compulsory	Yes/No
Statement of business	✓
Review of performance	✓
Prospects and impacts	✓

Material	
Management structure	✓
Shareholder returns	✓
Employment policies	✓
Environmental policies	✓
CSR policies	✓
Performance on employment, environment and CSR	✓
Reputation and other matters	✓

Comparison with industry indices (eg BITC Corporate Responsibility Index) and own success model.
Environment, Workplace, Community, Marketplace

Results
(including stakeholder audit)
Steps needed to meet OFR criteria and front-end reporting best practice

Stage 4

Task Force
Review effectiveness of stakeholder communication and the methods employed

Review
How could means of delivery and content be improved using OFR criteria and industry best-practice indices?

Report and accounts
Does it reflect the information needs highlighted in the stakeholder audit?
How does it compare with the best?
Does it satisfy OFR criteria?
Could front-end reporting be improved by dedicated section in the report and accounts or by separate reports?
Is the potential of the web being fully utilized?
Does the AGM need a re-think?
Is stakeholder communication 'joined-up' through formal and informal reporting?
Could public relations play a more effective oversight role?
Is the process independently audited?

Results
Reassurance that communications are stakeholder-driven and areas for improvement highlighted

Stage 5

Task Force
Implementation and monitoring for continuous improvement

Rolling monitor
Regular stakeholder audits provide rolling monitor of how well a company communicates the 'complete picture' – financial and non-financial
Publication of performance measures and indicators improves compatibility

Results
Greater understanding among stakeholders of financial and non-financial factors, their relationship and how they contribute to corporate reputation

The ingredients of the OFR

Draft OFR to Board

Source: CIPR (2002)

Key

Stage 1 Set up a cross-functional task force to head up the initiative, and carry out a review of the company's objectives and strategies to provide a 'success model' benchmark.

Stage 2 Identify stakeholders, internal as well as external. The OFR will broaden the role of the annual report and the range of stakeholders who will use it. Categorize audiences into primary and secondary. Conduct a stakeholder audit to discover what audiences know about the company, sources of information and nature of the relationship.

Stage 3 Compare the company's current reporting practice against OFR criteria, using a grid to identify information gaps, and against peer organizations via a range of available indices.

Stage 4 Review reporting methods and consider 'refreshing' reports, use of the web and format of the annual meeting.

Stage 5 Use the stakeholder audit as a rolling monitor of the effectiveness of non-financial reporting. The results of the methods used and outcomes should be published.

Figure 2.7 *An operating and financial review (OFR) matrix*

for and thus we see the recent rise in research and evaluation of corporate identity image and reputation. Brooking's (1996) classification of resources breaks down intellectual capital into market assets, human-centred assets, infrastructure assets and intellectual property assets. On the other hand, Quinn *et al* (1996) see professional intellect as operating on four levels of cognitive knowledge, advanced know-how, systems understanding and self-motivated creativity, which they regard as the highest level of intellect reflecting motivation and adaptability. Petrash (1996) described the approach to intellectual capital management adopted by the Dow Chemical Company by defining intellectual capital as a formula:

Intellectual capital = Human capital + Organizational capital + Customer capital.

Dow Chemical Company has over 75 multifunctional intellectual asset management teams that meet to review the patent portfolio. These are led by intellectual asset managers who in turn report to the intellectual management function. The whole is supported by an intellectual management centre that provides database support, career development of managers and sharing of best practice. What we are seeing then is a resource-driven approach to strategy based on the view that sustainable competitive advantage is derived from an identification of the firm's existing and future strategic capability. The long-term dynamic nature of a public relations strategy is that it is responsive to changes in the environment. It requires identifying existing and future communication gaps by sound professional public relations intellects, so that capability is underpinned by competence in the round.

Strategic alliances

Managing the public relations activity surrounding the outcomes of strategic alliances has become an important financial option for organizations. They involve relationships between organizations that fall short of merger but may go as far as mutual equity stakes, each organization owning a minority of shares in the other. On the other hand, they may involve no more than limited cooperation and consultation between otherwise bitter rivals, but either way the financial press will take a close interest. These alliances do not just involve very large organizations. No organization, whatever its size, can any longer hope to acquire all the skills and competencies necessary for operating in a global environment and it must therefore attempt to fill the gaps by working with other companies in partnership. The types of alliances that can arise are licences, joint ventures, franchising, private label agreements, buyer/seller arrangements or the forging of common standards and consortia. A prerequisite for a successful alliance is that there must be a clear purpose and objective for the arrangement and the process must be managed according to schedule and without loss of control. The role of the public relations strategist will be to ensure that media coverage does not lead to the organizations involved losing control of their own destinies.

It would be interesting to see how long the strategic alliance approach lasts. For example, there are already claims that Japanese companies rarely commit their best scientists and engineers to projects sponsored by the Ministry of International Trade and Industry (MITI), while IBM set up a special facility in Japan where Fujitsu could test its new mainframe software before considering a licensing agreement. This provided some protection against loss of technological know-how through an alliance. Brouthers (1995) outlines a set of guidelines to be considered, namely complementary skills, cooperative cultures, compatible goals and commensurate levels of risk – what he calls the Four Cs of successful international strategic alliances, as shown in the multinational giant Philips' alliance network and current joint ventures (2006); see Figure 2.8.

Figure 2.8 *Overview of Philips' strategic alliances*

Strategy in its classical sense is a competitive model that aims to enhance the value of an organization to its shareholders. An organization chooses between strategic options, which may include mergers and divestments. Public relations strategists may be involved in merger acquisitions to increase shareholder value, merger acquisitions' decision-making processes, post-merger implementations and corporate divestment programmes. Once an organization becomes too unwieldy from a communication perspective, it will need to segment its image and identity. Philips has 10 key joint ventures and participations and has segmented them into three key activity sectors.

The trend for sustainability, if not a reversal of the movement towards growth, has led to the break-up of some corporations with the intention of releasing shareholder value. In a turbulent environment, organizations have to include in their range of strategic options a consideration of unexpected as well as planned research and development. This is often seen as a cost rather than an investment in the UK and, as with public relations programmes, there are disagreements about the extent to which expenditure should be subjected to vigorous cost-benefit analysis. Given the emphasis on producing downsized companies and outsourcing many essential functions, including public relations, issues about innovation and the virtual company, Chesborough and Teece (1996) assert, are on the increase in many companies.

Crisis and resilience management

Restructuring during the 1980s and 1990s often saw functional areas such as investor relations and government relations become the remit of finance or treasury departments, while internal or employee management communication found itself positioned as a low priority activity in human resource departments. During a disaster, this often left responsibility for corporate affairs such as image, identity and reputation management in a vacuum and without reference to corporate PR and communication strategists other than as an afterthought by marketers responsible for customer relations or product promotion. The result was often a long-drawn-out damage limitation exercise, or worse.

The co-dependency Action Stations Framework (see Table 2.3) illustrates how emergency communication structures and processes are critical components in resilience planning. The role of corporate communication/ PR director is pivotal in any organization's continuity planning strategy, carrying much responsibility for optimum performance, board-level authority and accountability.

At this critical point in the history of corporate communication management theory and practice as it evolves from PR sector change and development in parallel with the convergence of technology, the role of integrated communication management in industry and commerce is once again attracting a higher profile, particularly in the banking industry, especially since the threats associated with the global economic recession. The principal activity during a crisis for communication specialists is likely to be media relations, yet titles and roles of communication practitioners in British organizations vary. In banks, for example, operational and strategic organizational functions, including crisis management, may appear as shown in Table 2.3 although, as we went to press, this may be changing as a result of the credit crunch limitations on lending and other financial services.

Table 2.3 *Operational PR functions in banks*

Banks	Department	Functions
Abbey National	Corporate Affairs	Media relations; public relations; internal communication (newsletter, video)
Barclays Bank	Communications	Shareholder communications; press relations
Co-operative Bank	Public Relations	Press information; opinion survey; publicity; policy development; community projects; funding for charity works; internal communications
Lloyds Bank	Corporate Communications	Environmental policy; community support; internal communication; information service to the public, in particular students; corporate sponsorship; press information
Midland Bank	Corporate Communications	Monitor corporate identity; corporate brochure; internal communication; media relations, public relations; ethnic and environmental policy

Organization	Department	Activities
NatWest Bank	Corporate Affairs & Communications	Coordinate internal communication; group media relations; develop public and ethnical business policies; investor relations; community relations; campaign for plain English; 'green policy' – best practice; staff suggestion scheme; school programme – financial literacy, personal money management, opinion formers (politicians, business leaders) relations; advise business unit on advertising
Royal Bank of Scotland	Corporate Communications	Community relations; corporate sponsorship of sport and cultural events; environmental policy – energy conservation; guides to services and products
TSB Bank	Group Corporate Communications	Corporate advertising; press relations; investor relations; corporate identity; internal communication – newsletter and special events
British Bankers Association	Communications and External Affairs	Communication strategy; media relations; 'educating' the public; identify target audience; opinion research; banking seminar and conferences

Back in 1986, a Gallup survey of Britain showed that only 3 per cent of the general population trusted bankers. In today's crisis situation, banks are likely to attract more adverse publicity from the media than other professions. Although Liew's research in 1997 indicated that Britons were largely satisfied with the performance of the banks and were less antagonistic than the media indicates today, an integrated communication strategy is more than ever essential in managing relationships with all stakeholders. Liew writes, 'effective relationship management requires corporate action or change. Corporate communication – including the research function – plays a role in shaping a bank's course of action, how it is structured and its decision-making process.'

Banks perhaps more than most have had to address the sheer scale of environmental change brought about by technology, globalization and social change, so although Liew found no significant anti-bank bias in the media, he argued that 'the weakness in existing bank/media relations in the United Kingdom is a glaring knowledge gap that will expand as the nature of banking business increases in complexity' (1982).

Public relations, by definition, has always had the notion of symmetrical communication at the heart of 'best practice', but technological advancement now limits the concept. Today, asymmetrical communication takes relationship management to new levels of sophistication and quality control.

Thus tactical, empirically derived evidence for communication programme planning and budgeting is no longer good enough. Strategy informs tactics at both research planning and evaluation levels to a very high degree, which is why corporate communication studies at Thames Valley University Faculty of Professional Studies in London was one of the first in Europe to incorporate knowledge and information management as a core learning module in its Master's degree programme, in addition to the ability to critically analyse best practice models of strategic PR performance and one-off PR campaigns.

What the books say

Given the limitations of empirical research underpinning the professional era of public relations between the post-war period and the present day, academics have attempted to apply business or corporate strategy models to the management of communication as a value-added component of linked organizational mission and goals. However, awareness of the need for companies and investors to maintain relationships with all stakeholders in the interests of corporate performance puts pressure on companies to reassess levels of influence that could be reliably measured in respect of the bottom line. Gaved (1997) argued that:

a new model of corporate change and evolution needs to be developed, which enables management teams to be renewed without major discontinuity. This need is quite independent of the issue of takeovers. What we currently have is a system of informal influence, which increases the pressures on companies – which normally means the CEO and chairpersons – in response to deterioration of performance. For most companies, most of the time there is very little of this 'behind closed doors' influence, but when it does take place, it is the largest shareholders who get most involved and who have disproportionate influence on the company, board and senior management team.

Although there can be no one universal model for coping with crises, Table 2.4 identifies and distinguishes the difference between routine emergencies and disasters. For an international bank experiencing, say, cyberspace terrorism as a result of systems intervention from a hostile hacker, dependency on a geographical measure to define the scale of such crisis is unlikely to be very helpful. Prior to the mid-1980s, PR practitioners thought in terms of 'routine emergencies' and suggested that a crisis has five stages. Fearn-Banks argued that crisis management is strategic planning to prevent and respond during a crisis or negative occurrence, a process that removes some of the risk and uncertainty and allows the organization to be in greater control of its density. However, if as she says a crisis has five stages, the banking culture has to create for itself an anticipatory model of crisis management that 'guides practitioners toward a position in which they can proactively investigate their organization to determine the most likely cause of technological crisis'. With a foundation in anticipation and empowerment, each bank's model would optimize the precautionary abilities of the organization to prevent and cope with a crisis or 'routine emergency', but would they be adequate for a 'disaster'? Table 2.5 shows the number and type of international terrorist incidents in the 10 years to 1979.

Olaniran and Williams (2001) argue that 'crisis prevention requires a thorough understanding of the technology and the context in which the technology is being used'. This includes processes of enactment and expectation as well as vigilant decision making, and they suggest there are two key issues involved, namely rigidity and control.

Rigidity is the degree of inflexibility built into a particular action or process. This is important in terms of interaction and successful outcome because it recognizes that individuals will view problems during any crisis in different ways; through different perceptions people select different options from those available and the consequences will determine the quality of the outcome. Control on the other hand is viewed as 'the degree of influence that organizational members have at their disposal. Control is often elusive because it has to do with individual perception especially

Table 2.4 *Differences between routine emergencies and disasters*

Routine emergencies	Disasters
Interaction with familiar faces	Interaction with unfamiliar faces
Familiar tasks and procedures	Unfamiliar tasks and procedures
Intra-organizational coordination needed	Intra- and inter-organizational coordination needed
Roads, telephones, facilities intact	Roads blocked or jammed, telephones jammed or non-functional, facilities damaged
Communications frequencies adequate for radio traffic	Radio frequencies often overloaded
Communication intra-organizational	Need for inter-organizational information sharing
Use of familiar terminology in communicating	Communication with persons who use different terminology or speak another language
Need to deal mainly with local press	Hordes of national and international reporters
Management structure adequate to coordinate the number of resources involved	Resources often exceed management capacity

Source: Aufderheide (1999)

when the influence is indirect in nature.' Olaniran and Williams quote the case of ATAT's crisis episode in which 'a software glitch caused a power outage that disrupted its nationwide services for nine hours in January 1990', causing 'an inter-dependent effect on other organizations'. The authors suggest that the anticipatory model of management can be likened to the law of probability indicating that the less frequent the occurrence of an event, the greater the probability that the event will occur in the future. Therefore, organizations should and must continue to evaluate reliance on technology and to prepare for crises in advance. The anticipatory model of crisis management suggests the possibility that crises could be held in

Table 2.5 *International terrorism incidents, 1968–79*

	Number	*%*
Type		
Explosive bombings	1,588	48
Incendiary bombings	456	14
Kidnappings	263	8
Assassinations	246	7
Armed attacks	188	6
Letter bombings	186	6
Hijackings	100	3
Theft/break-ins	78	2
Barricade and hostage	73	2
Snipings	71	2
Other	87	3
Target		
Business executives/facilities	487	36
Diplomatic officials/property	273	20
Other government officials	217	16
Military officials/property	204	15
Private citizens	166	12

Source: US Department of Defense and Central Intelligence Agency, in Regester (1989)

check through an understanding of preconditions and instituting action plans to counteract the precondition effects.

'In nearly every global disaster situation, it is the case that at some level or another, information was available which could have prevented the disaster from happening', wrote Allison in 1993. However, he argued, the information was either possessed by those with authority to act upon it, but who did not act; or it was not possessed by those with the authority to act and it was not sought out by those in authority; or it was possessed by those who did not have the power to act on it, but not shared by them with the parties who did possess the authority to act upon it; or it was shared with the parties who possessed the authority to act on it, but the parties with the requisite authority did not take the information seriously enough. Thus the will to communicate relies to some extent on the existing culture of the organization and its available expertise not only in speaking and providing information through the media during the crisis and afterwards, but also in taking responsibility for ensuring free-flowing information through the proper application of continuity plans.

This responsibility relies heavily on an understanding of the chain of command when the informal system of influence mentioned earlier is clearly inappropriate due to the impact of uncontrollable time constraints. During a crisis and particularly during a disaster, each individual in the communication operational chain must know to whom she or he is responsible and there should be units of different managerial sizes of different purposes and all units will have simulated and practised under health and safety regulations. Clearly this span of control must not be excessive, but must be organized so that real control is maintained like an army in war time. In other words, the open system of normal management practice will click into a closed system based on military-style organization and coordination principles. In wider civilian terms where organizations must liaise with local authorities, this means that the scalar concept that views an organization as a group of grades arranged in sequence with the superior grades carrying authority and the lower grades carrying no authority, becomes irrelevant. The unity of command will belong to the people trained as members of special emergency communication and continuity planning teams.

On 19 June 2003 the British government's Cabinet Office released a draft 'Civil Contingencies Bill'. For the first time this provides a single statutory framework for civil protection and emergency planning in the United Kingdom, imposing a duty to undertake risk assessments in respect of emergency planning. In the last six years, in response to civil rights organizations and local authorities, the British Government has tightened its definition of 'emergency'. At local authority level, a major emergency plan (MEP) has been drafted in accordance with the agreed procedures and practices given in the Major Incident Procedures Manual published by the London Emergency Services Liaison Panel (LESLP). The manual is made available to all on the Metropolitan Police website.

The MEP provides guidance to those responsible for managing and co-ordinating the council response to a major emergency. It is geared towards the setting up of the Emergency Coordination Centre and the roles of key personnel, internally and externally. Due to the wide range of circumstances that a council or local authority may be called upon to deal with, it is neither event- nor site-specific, but is generic in nature. The flexibility that this approach assumes has stood the test of time.

The MEP is supported by a department emergency plan, which outlines the procedures to be adopted within each department. Those departmental plans and those of their contractor partners standardize the layout and ensure a corporate style which everyone understands. MEP and departmental plans are reviewed annually.

For a local authority a major emergency exists where the required council response, at the scene or elsewhere, is in excess of that which can be provided by the council operating under normal conditions and/or where special mobilization and organization of council services is necessary.

Many emergencies are dealt with by departments under their own departmental emergency arrangements, without the need to activate the major emergency plan. However, whilst events that occur during normal working hours may be dealt with perfectly adequately from available resources, the same event arising during the early hours of the morning, or at the weekend, may require a major emergency response due to the reduced resources immediately available to deal with it.

Back in 1916, the concept of forecast plans was called 'purveyance' by Fayol who saw it as one of five divisions of the administrative function, while administration was one of six operations to be found in a business, the other five being technical, commercial, financial, security and accounting. Together these activities are what today we term 'management'. However, Fayol could never have imagined the complexity of currently managing organizations where routine organizational activities are disrupted not only internally, but externally by what Florence and Kovacic (2001) call 'the interconnected actions of the major stakeholders' and when 'organizational crisis truly become the public concern when defined and influenced by the mass media'. They quote Thurow's conceptual framework of 'punctuated equilibrium', which depicts an organization's crisis as 'rapid developments characterized by flux, disequilibrium and uncertainty'. Zhu and Blood (1997) offer a four-stage universal model:

1. The build up or pre-crisis period, where the symptoms are detectable, such as repeated messages or persistent sets of clues.
2. Crisis breakout – the initial stage is the acute phase.
3. Abatement or chronicity of the crisis with charges, counter-charges, demonstrations, inquiries, legal actions and the continuing coverage by the mass media.
4. Termination, where the organization attempts to get back to normal and where the crisis is no longer a threat to an organization's operational environment or its constituent publics. The media set the agenda in terms of communication during the crisis lifecycle.

Third parties, such as the media, play a key role in assessing risk, which evolves from research and corporate intelligence. This requires a high degree of trust and confidence. Back in 1995 public confidence in scientists working for industry was only 64 per cent; media confidence in scientists working for industry was only 38 per cent, suggested Ipsos MORI to the CIPR. Today, there is considerable media speculation as the result of technological developments of the internet, such as social networking. The public relations industry is accelerating its research development needs in the light of advancing telecommunications such as mobile phones, iPods and other devices. This is taking place mainly through PR techniques and evaluation measures of trust and confidence either in-house or third party information expertise. The challenge for industry, central or local government communicators, is how to evaluate both symmetrical and asymmetrical information.

However, trust is usually a symmetrical or two-way process, top down and bottom up. The PR practitioner role is to present on behalf of his or her masters, so there is no room for naivety. Trust is a duty of care on the part of both parties. The PR practitioner has to have unconditional confidence in management pronouncements and demands.

The UK's Institute for Public Policy Research declares that 'modern intelligence access ... may have to be at the expense of some aspects of privacy', which is a human right under the European Convention except at times of national security and emergencies. Government access would be provided by 'data-mining' and processing techniques used to analyse personal information at any time. While the government's role in national security is generally recognized, the public fears this threatens democracy as it has known it. Indeed, one British journalist wrote 'if no communication is private, no confidential source will ever speak to a journalist again'. The implications inherent in such technological developments place a greater burden of trust on everyone, but especially on the PR practitioner who will need to remain ever vigilant in terms of complicity or otherwise, in what is said and done, or not, in the name of public relations.

Managerial perception

Communications managers often confuse risk assessment with risk perception during message design and implementation (Susskind and Field, 1996). Perception plays an important part at every stage of monitoring and evaluation of public response. For example, Susskind and Field (in Florence and Kovacic, 2001: 84) suggest six types of anger requiring different responses, namely: when people have been hurt; when people feel threatened by risks not of their own making; when people feel their fundamental beliefs are being challenged; when people feel weak in the face of powerful others; when people believe they have been lied to or duped; and when people strategically display anger to manipulate the reactions of others.

Thus, confidence in the quality of information provision and in the perceptions of management relies on what Sopow (1994) calls the critical issues audit based on recognition of the main points (recognizable in key phrases such as unique, new, first, only or last); in quality support through research, evidence, studies and testing methods; and through public linkages that emerge through what people say, what the public demands and strong support (Regester and Larkin, 1997: 32). UK consultants Regester and

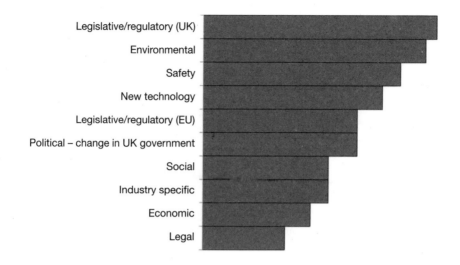

Legislative/regulatory (UK)
Environmental
Safety
New technology
Legislative/regulatory (EU)
Political – change in UK government
Social
Industry specific
Economic
Legal

Source: Regester and Larkin (1997)

Figure 2.9   *Information costs and choices*

Larkin's 1995 UK research audit suggests the organizational priorities based on cost and choice shown in Figure 2.9. A 1994 survey of 250 British companies indicated that employees thought a crisis was more likely to be triggered from outside the organization, rather than inside by management, as shown in Figure 2.10.

Florence and Kovacic (2001) suggest three models of crisis communication management. Their marketplace model argues that crises are caused and solved by economic, political and legal competition; ideologically based models evolving new or evolving social movements; and a public participation model based on cooperation among governments, private industry and the public. Because of the significance of mass media involvement, these authors stress the importance of message strategies; by identifying stages in a crisis, message strategies can be more appropriately put together, up to a point. Of course, unknown variables make a positive risk-theoretical view virtually impossible and so as with the model of forecasting, empirical knowledge is built up with experience so that an understanding of the 'probabilities consequent to certain actions' takes place. The media affect people's perception during the very first moments that they see or hear about a crisis and so one aspect is indisputable. The facts have to be reliable and the attitude credible no matter how different the communication code systems and styles are.

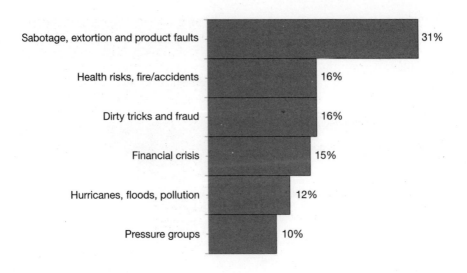

Figure 2.10 *Likely causes of crises before recession*

The literature up to the mid-1980s focuses on tactical PR activities and to a lesser extent on PR strategy as organizations became increasingly technologically dependent. But something else happened in the United Kingdom to create a paradigm shift and it began with issues around corporate governance.

Corporate governance

With the rise of banks and other organizations as techno-organizations, the significance of corporate governance is a popular media topic. Williams (1997) suggests that directors' oaths would consist of sets of statements to:

> reflect the director's strong commitment to his or her employees, the top priority of safety, the high ethical importance of communication and the protection of that communication. A director's oath might include statements that he or she as director is morally responsible for seeing to it that both a will to communicate and a structure for communication are present in the organizations.

Ten years earlier, Allison had suggested 'the establishment of a tenured, independently funded safety board which would possess veto power over operational decisions which placed the lives of employees or the general public at risk'. Allison's views were based on all of the disasters he studied where a serious communication breakdown occurred during the crisis which had been openly acknowledged by 'totally separate judges and investigative committees'.

The Institute of Chartered Accountants in England and Wales (ICAEW) established the Turnbull Working Party to provide assistance to companies in implementing internal control requirements including crisis management strategies; a report was drafted in April 1999, published on 28 September 1999 and became a statutory requirement in December 2000. It represents the final element in a combined code on corporate governance, and full compliance with the code became a requirement for listed companies from 23 December 2000. The combined code incorporates the Turnbull Report, the Cadbury Report and the Hampel Report and suggests key performance indicators as follows:

- obtain management cooperation;
- prepare a plan;
- identify objectives;
- prioritize the risk to the achievement of the above objectives;
- establish a risk management policy;
- consult through the organization;
- improve the culture of the organization, where and if appropriate;
- keep the whole plan simple and straightforward;
- monitor;
- incorporate the Turnbull plan in the organization's management and corporate governance processes.

The author of the Report, Nigel Turnbull, states:

> we have focused on producing practical guidance that will ensure that the board is aware of the significant risks faced by their company and procedures in place to manage them. Executive management is responsible for managing risks through maintaining an effective system of internal control and the board as whole is responsible for reporting on it.

Public Limited Companies are expected to have a solid internal control system to safeguard the investments of shareholders and the assets of the company.

The effectiveness of internal controls has to be reviewed at least once a year and the risks and issues a business faces should be regularly evaluated. Risk management, operation and compliance and financial controls should be part of a company's review and the entire board of directors is responsible for risk management. An organization has to keep under review the requirement of an internal audit department and the contingency plan of the Turnbull Report was put together so companies can focus on internal controls and specifically their crisis management programme. The report states that 'social and environmental factors should be included in risk assessments along with conventional/financial threats'. The report also recommends that listed companies radically review their risk management programmes. Thus Nick Bent of Burson-Marsteller, a large PR consultancy, stated:

> the Turnbull Report means that companies will have to take a broad, sophisticated approach to risk, explicitly including environmental matters and threats to reputation. Reputation is a key element of the intangible assets of a company and hence its value.

The Turnbull Report encompasses issues relating to electronic media now that stakeholders expect and demand information in real time and e-mail has raised the expectations of shareholders regarding how quickly companies respond. A typical contingency plan to meet the demands of the Turnbull Report can be seen from Accenture's business risk management process:

- establish goals;
- assessment of the risk;
- develop risk solutions;
- design and implement controls;
- monitor and feedback;
- improve the process.

For these stages to be successful Accenture notes that the quality of information is crucial for sound decision making. Each of the stages must 'generate and use time relevant and reliable information'.

Crisis management specialists, Regester and Larkin, state:

> in today's complex environment, organizations have to understand and respond rapidly to shifting public values, rising expectations, demands for public consultation and an increasingly intrusive news-media. This is particularly crucial when things go wrong.

Brian O'Connell, writing in the *Investor Relations Journal*, suggests 'the internet has an estimated 2 billion pages of information and is growing at a pace of 100 million pages per month'. The main crisis arising from this trend is the growth of bulletin boards or chat rooms. It is now possible for an individual to post any sort of information, accurate or inaccurate, on one of these sites and spear illicit and inaccurate information about the company and the management. This suggests the need for these sites to be monitored closely and outsourcing companies now exist who will undertake search and monitoring on behalf of organizations such as banks. The Investor Relations Society recognizes best practice in its web guidelines. For example, PR practitioners know that mishandling bad news creates a crisis of confidence in the ability of a company to manage its affairs properly. The result can be disastrous for investors, employees and customers; in some cases a company may never recover. The Society recognizes that it is the responsibility of the communication department to handle events in a professional manner.

The London Stock Exchange points to two levels to crisis management. The first level is where a company should look for anything within its business that may cause a crisis; the second concerns preparation for specific issues. For example, where a bank may be in the middle of talks about a takeover or merger with another bank, it should be assumed this news will be leaked to the media. This sort of issue is relatively predictable and therefore plenty of preparation should and could be undertaken in the form of pre-prepared or holding statements for the press and other media groups and preparations and training of management on what to do and say when approached by the media or other parties requesting information. In a report by the UK Department of Trade and Industry 'Creating Quality Dialogue' (1998) it was stated that only 21 per cent of fund managers think that smaller quoted companies, for example, are proficient at communicating information. Imagine how much worse that could be during a crisis.

The organizational crisis matrix in Figure 2.11 suggests the extent to which different parties have control over different types of crises at any given point in time. Each of the crises listed has the potential to damage an organization's reputation if the amount of control a company has over the outcome of different types of crises is not recognized; understood and addressed accordingly.

The Financial Standard Authority (FSA) states in rule 39:

> a firm should have in place appropriate arrangements, having regard to the scale, nature and complexity of its business, to ensure that it can continue to function and meets its regulatory obligations in the event of an unforeseen interruption. These arrangements should be regularly updated and tested to ensure their effectiveness.

Companies face increasing regulation concerning disclosure of information, which if not handled competently by corporate communication experts will attract attention during a crisis from financial journalists and other interested parties. For example, the Y2K Regulation Fair Disclosure (Reg. FD) prohibits selective disclosure and requires the simultaneous disclosure of material information to the general public with disclosure to analysts or any other group. The aim is to ensure a fair and consistent flow of information to all stakeholder groups where previously certain parties

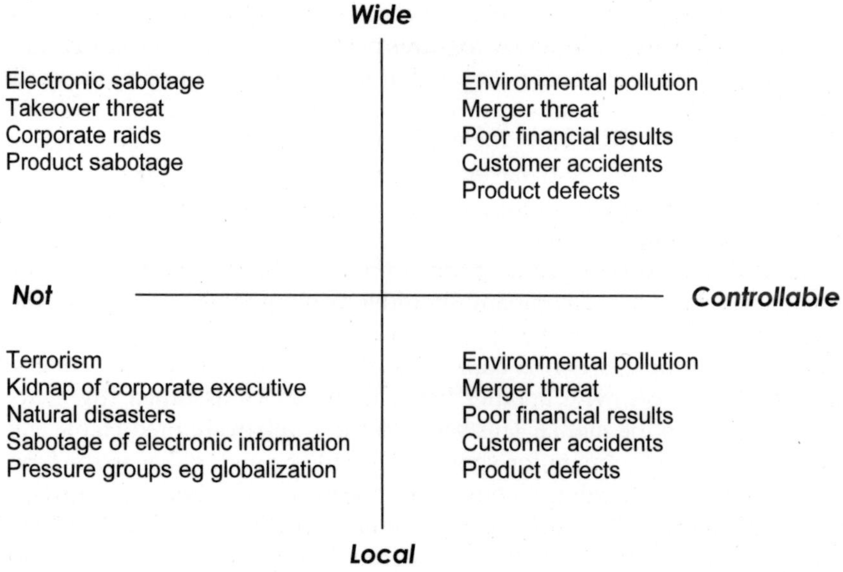

Wide

Electronic sabotage	Environmental pollution
Takeover threat	Merger threat
Corporate raids	Poor financial results
Product sabotage	Customer accidents
	Product defects

Not ──────────────────────────── **Controllable**

Terrorism	Environmental pollution
Kidnap of corporate executive	Merger threat
Natural disasters	Poor financial results
Sabotage of electronic information	Customer accidents
Pressure groups eg globalization	Product defects

Local

Source: Adapted from Fill (1999)

Figure 2.11   *A crisis impact model*

received privileged information from which they accrued considerable advantage. It also aims to discourage 'mosaic' information, which the UK Financial Services Authority describes as 'information which, when pieced together with other like matter, creates a material insight into the affairs of a company'. This carries considerable significance after a crisis and for its reporting in a company's quarterly review and annual report and accounts.

Continuity planning

It is interesting looking through the case studies on business continuity planning websites such as Global Continuity.com to observe how only now are organizations beginning to understand that even though many may have continuity plans in place, the strategic and operational demands being placed on human corporate communication in the event of an invocation are not being addressed (Figure 2.12).

Crisis management is often referred to as issues management by organizations in order for a threat to appear less dramatic to prevent overreaction by the media and panic by susceptible stakeholders (see Table 2.6). The

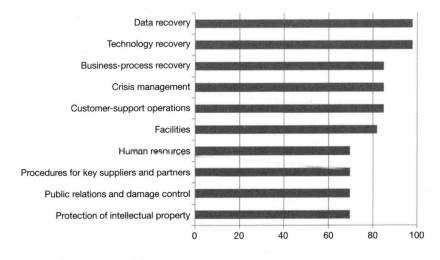

Source: Luftman (2003: 164)

Figure 2.12 *Elements of a business continuity plan (BCP)*

most frequent potential crises many industries face, especially the banking industry, are computer viruses, with the fear that one might cause the collapse of all computer systems throughout the world. The Y2K crisis failed to materialize, but large sums of money were spent by companies panicked into putting contingency plans in place. This involved emergency

Table 2.6 *Nine steps to managing BCP performance*

1. *Visualize* the business functions (top-down approach)
2. *Itemize* the tasks involved (bottom-up approach)
3. *Prioritize* work only on critical functions until they are substantially complete
4. *Categorize* and organize the problems into management pieces of work
5. *Minimize* the risk – the ultimate goal of business continuity planning
6. *Organize* staff to react to emergencies as they occur
7. *Rehearse* events so that staff are familiar with the planned responses
8. *Sponsor/champion* participation to demonstrate and communicate the importance of the recovery plan
9. *Vigilant* monitoring of supply chain and partners' plans

Source: Giga Group in Luftman (2003)

training of staff and paying overtime rates to IT employees for holiday pay. One Canadian bank, for example, held a full day simulation in its residential training centre where nearly 500 senior staff participated. It used two of its PR staff to simulate the press, complete with professional video camera to inject a level of realism into the situation and to provide a tool for use at subsequent debriefings via their own training video.

Luftman (2003) argues that 'recovery and management plans should be tested at least annually or twice yearly, with performance of electrical supplies, voice and data communications experts, transit systems for staff, building, heating and air conditioning experts, elevator or lift service companies' (Figure 2.12).

Another area of concern during the Y2K 'crisis' was public perception. Although the industry appeared to be on top of the problem, naturally banks could not anticipate the degree to which the public might draw out cash and overload individual bank's ability to respond. The Canadian Bankers Association, traditionally a low-profile damage control type of organization, became proactive in developing a strategy to make sure it had well briefed representatives wherever banking issues of Y2K were likely to be discussed, whether in the national media or in schools. It developed a new website and issued explanatory leaflets through its Y2K public affairs working group. While one of the benefits of new technology has been the 24/7 facility that databases provide via websites, cyberspace can also be a threat. While the internet may be a useful monitoring tool for information gathering, it also creates narrow costing and a demand for highly skilled practitioners who can monitor and disseminate proactively to produce critical intelligence that will affect an organization's reputation or security.

For example, the fastest growing crime in the United Kingdom currently is identity fraud. The UK fraud prevention service, CIFAS, reported 75,000 cases in 2002 alone, an increase of 55,000 in just three years. CIFAS has revealed some interesting gender patterns, with the proportion of female fraudsters most often noted in mail order, communications and loan frauds, while the majority of male fraudsters are most often noted in the areas of assets, finance and insurance. Richard Hurley, CIFAS Communications Manager, concludes on his 2009 website, 'what should never be forgotten, however, is the damage ... in terms of financial loss and professional reputation'. With call centres increasing in number and moved to economically weaker countries, the longer-term implications are clear. UK bank accounts will be hard for internal and external fraudsters to resist if sophisticated 'man and machine' security measures are not embedded in corporate communication plans underpinning continuity planning training policies.

Corporate communication lies at the heart of all commercial operational activity, but especially where organizational security is concerned. This demands excellence in internal communication practices from the top, as well

CONTINUITY PR MANAGEMENT: A training matrix

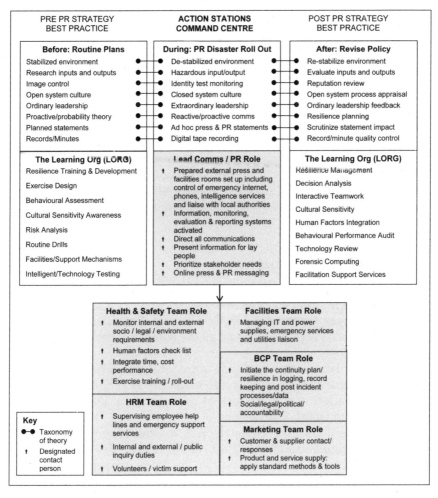

Source: Adapted from the Action Stations Framework, Oliver (2004)

Figure 2.13   *Crisis and resilience: communication infrastructure*

as excellence in driving external PR programming and everyday corporate affairs. An organizational climate and training that can demonstrate that its people work well together and stay together during a crisis, overcomes setbacks more quickly (see Figure 2.13). Internal strife or unethical behaviour can rarely be dissociated from an organizational culture that may have preceded or triggered a crisis in the first place, but effective training is the key to resilience.

CAMPAIGN: THE PARTNERSHIP OF DISASTER RESPONSE, UNITED STATES

Disasters create physical, financial and emotional crises that require quick, decisive action from many entities. Business leaders have been generous in responding to disasters, but they often struggle to determine how best to contribute.

In order to strengthen the private sector's response to disasters, the Business Roundtable, a membership organization of 160 CEOs from leading companies, worked with Edelman to launch a new initiative – the Partnership for Disaster Response – to expand corporate commitment beyond financial contributions and to create an educational resource for companies.

Challenge vs opportunity

During a disaster, there is often a lack of clarity about who is in charge. The government, relief agencies and the private sector cannot manage the complexity of a catastrophe each on its own. The first challenge the Partnership faced was to coordinate all the different sectors involved in disaster response.

Moreover, there is often confusion about what is truly needed after a disaster. Companies were often unable to get critical information during the 2005 disasters due to the lack of relationships in place with key government and relief organizations.

The Partnership's third challenge was to streamline the business community's response and integrate it into the nation's disaster response plans. The success of the Partnership would be measured by how well it developed plans and protocols to help mitigate each of these challenges.

Research

The Partnership conducted extensive primary and secondary research to evaluate the current landscape, shape the strategic focus, and develop areas of collaboration with other disaster response entities.

Secondary research

The Partnership evaluated numerous government, academic and think-tank reports as well as ongoing media coverage to identify key lessons learnt from the 2005 disasters and understand how it could improve collaboration among the different entities involved in disaster response. The key findings from the research include:

- There was a lack of information and poor communications about what is needed on the ground from the business community.
- Businesses have a dual role in disaster preparedness and response.
- The next major catastrophic disaster could result in economic damage over $100 billion.
- The national must adopt a 'culture of preparedness'.

Private sector

The Partnership organized quarterly meetings throughout the year to understand concerns about the private sector's role in disasters and identify gaps. The most common findings included the:

- lack of useful information in the different phases of disasters;
- absence of relationships in place prior to disasters;
- lack of understanding of the private sector's capabilities during a disaster;
- need to coordinate and streamline the private sector's communication during disasters in order not to duplicate response efforts.

NGOs

The Partnership organized a series of meetings with non-profits to see how to forge stronger partnerships between sectors. The key finding was that relief agencies wanted the private sector to share its expertise and be part of the planning process – especially in the areas of logistics and communications.

Strategic plan

Developing objectives

- Develop an infrastructure to support the response to catastrophic disasters.
- Educate relief agencies, business associations, government and the general public about how to leverage the private sector's resources and expertise during a disaster.
- Galvanize the business community to work together in a coordinated, effective manner.
- Serve as a model and reference for other businesses, NGOs, the government and media in disaster preparedness and response.

Determining target audiences

- Business community.
- NGOs/relief agencies.
- Government.

Developing communication messages and criteria for success

- Develop a central repository of information to help the business community better prepare and respond to disasters.
- Foster partnerships to effectively integrate the private sector into the nation's response plan.
- Develop communication plans, protocols and tools to share information and coordinate the private sector's response to disasters.

Operational strategy

1. Developed an educational website to serve as a central repository of information: www.respondtodisaster.org is the first comprehensive clearinghouse of information that leverages cross-industry expertise to help the business community prepare for and respond to disasters.
2. Developed resource guide throughout all phases of disaster response and distributed the materials to key disaster decision makers from business, government and NGOs. Materials included: Family Preparedness Guide; Guide to help HR leaders support employees who have been affected by a disaster; A guide for security, real estate, tax and legal staff on issues to consider when sharing office space after a disaster; Rebuilding communities; The Dos and Don'ts of effective giving; How can my company help?; Top Ten myths of disaster relief.
3. Created a formal partnership with the American Red Cross. The size and scale of this partnership is truly unique in that it is aligning the nation's largest companies with the nation's largest relief agency to create a stronger disaster response system and serve as a model programme for other businesses and NGOs.
4. Created emergency protocols to strengthen communications between the business community and relief agencies at the time of a disaster. These detailed action plans are the first ever attempt to codify how businesses will coordinate with each other, the American Red Cross and a coalition of seven of the largest humanitarian relief agencies (World Vision, CARE, Catholic Relief Services, International

Rescue Committee, Mercy Corps, Oxfam and Save the Children) during a national or international disaster.
5. Developed a secure web portal and phone line for member companies to communicate critical information and needs during a disaster. These tools allow the business community to quickly galvanize and determine how they can effectively leverage their resources to speed the response effort and help communities in need.
6. Developed a crisis plan to prepare to communicate effectively and efficiently in the event of a catastrophic disaster. This plan will enable the private sector to keep the media, families and communities up-to-date on the private sector's contributions and activities to help speed the relief effort.

Campaign outcomes

The visibility and profile of the Partnership as the leading business organ- ization on disaster response was raised as evidenced by its acceptance and connection with top humanitarian agencies (as rated by Charity Navigator) on all matters related to disasters.

The Partnership's infrastructure to support the response effort for catastrophic disasters was tested during the 2007 wildfires in southern California. The Partnership was immediately able to mobilize its members and, to date, the members have donated more than US$2.5 million in financial and in-kind contributions to reduce the impact of the disaster.

The Partnership for Disaster Response's website (www. respondtodisaster.org) was used extensively by companies and NGOs to share best practices in disaster response. The website has received more than 657,000 hits to date, a 470 per cent increase over 2006. The website has received extensive praise from the business community (SAP Americas, Procter & Gamble), NGOs (CARE and American Red Cross), government (Department of Homeland Security and FEMA), academia (George Washington University) and other key stakeholders.

The Partnership for Disaster Response has received positive media attention on its activities and achievements. To date, the Partnership has generated over 200 million media impressions from top media outlets including: AP, Bloomberg TV, *Chronicle of Philanthropy*, CNN, *Congressional Quarterly*, *Dallas Morning News*, *Financial Times*, *Forbes*, *Fortune*, *Harvard Business Review*, *HS Today*, *Investors Business Daily*, *Newsweek*, *Security Management*, *USA Today*, *Wall Street Journal* and *Washington Post*.

REFLECTION

Based on the information provided:

1. Do you think that different tools and techniques are required for The Partnership of Disaster Response and if so, by applying Figures 2.5 and 2.8 to private sector and public NGO sector PR, discuss what they are and why?
2. Who were the boundary spanners at the Partnership?
3. By focusing on Figures 2.6 and 2.7 and given the sensitivity of the subject matter, what processes helped to manage and control hotline and website traffic?
4. Was ordinary or extraordinary management of the PR campaign a contributory factor in its success?
5. What intangible assets are likely to add value to the relief agencies and how could they be reported and measured as tangible outcomes?

3

REPUTATION MANAGEMENT:
A celebrity-driven society

The public relations profession operates in a celebrity-driven world where even business leaders are groomed for public acceptability and promoted as icons. Public relations practitioners are often confused and bemused by the links between corporate image, corporate identity and reputation, but it is clear that the accumulation of empirical research on corporate image formation has led to the corporate identity literature of today.

The following definitions are adapted from current English usage in *Collins English Dictionary:*

Celebrity: Fame or notoriety.
Image: A mental picture or idea produced from imagination or personality and presented by the public to/of a person, group or organization by others.
Identity: A state of having unique identifying or individual characteristics by which a person or thing recognizes or defines him/her/itself.
Reputation: Notoriety or fame, especially for some specified positive or negative characteristic. Repute is the public estimation of a person or thing to be as specified, usually passive.

Corporate image

Image has had a bad press in public relations terms, yet image consultants continue to be in great demand. There are a number of reasons for this. The technological era has made people everywhere aware of, if not educated about, the roles of government and big business in society. Organizations today have become sensitive to the fact that corporate image operates in different dimensions for different audiences, to arrive as close as possible to what Boorstin (1963) describes as pseudo-ideal, which must be synthetic, believable, passive, vivid and ambiguous. Part of the bad press may lie in the fact that image can be as abstract a concept as Boorstin suggests and therefore lays itself open to suspicion. Bernstein (1991) calls it a vaporous concept of imprecise language, superficial thinking and self-styled image makers who contribute to the insubstantiality. However, Mackiewicz (1993) believes that a strong corporate image is an essential asset in today's era of borderless competition and argues, so what? However nebulous, image is reality because people can only react to what they experience and perceive. Rogers (1993) said, 'I do not react to some abstract reality but to my perception of this reality. It is this perception which for me is reality.'

Thus the nature of corporate image itself, however unpalatable, remains a growth area of public relations activity which, in combination with a growing body of knowledge about stakeholder expectation and cultural diversity, remains a popular focus of interest. Even companies that prefer to adopt a low profile are assessing their corporate image and its significance when studying their stakeholders' perceptions of their company policies, procedures and behaviour. Other writers find that the low profile most usually associated with such companies evokes words such as 'avoidance', 'uninvolved', 'passive', 'yielding' and 'not influential', and companies may spend as much time and money on maintaining their low profile as they could maintaining a higher one.

Belief systems play a part in people's attitudes. Unfavourable beliefs can lead to a drop in sales or a lowering of share price, which can be corrected by public relations involvement. Many writers and practitioners argue that beliefs make up product and brand images and that people act on those images. The checks and balances in any strategic campaign allow for modification of organizational behaviour or public perception to adjust knowledge, feelings or belief accordingly. Writing during the same period, Eiser suggested that a situation in which there is no communication loop between individuals' expressed attitudes and their behaviour will lead to a situation where stakeholders can only communicate their preferences through actions rather than words.

More current studies show that image does not consist of a single reality held by individuals, but that they hold a series of linked pictures consisting of many elements or objects that merge together and are interpreted through language.

Image and branding

Corporate image in the professional public relations sense goes back to the 1950s and the introduction of new commercial television stations. Marketing firms jumped on the bandwagon of creating brand image without any systematic theoretical foundation, so that people like Newman (1956) reported that 'the business firm may have nobody to be kicked but it does have a character'. Boulding (1956) said, 'the relationship between corporate image and the behaviour of the consumers, saying that what the individual, especially a celebrity on television, believed to be true, was true for him'.

When advertisers picked up the notion of image as a tool for branding products as well as corporate identity, writers of the day like Mayer (1961) saw the brand as a visible status symbol. Thirty years later Gorb (1992) was to argue that the business of corporate image design had become trivialized by too close association with external visual symbolism like logos. He recognized that the dynamics of image lie within the firm itself and have as much to do with manners and interrelationships as with markets. Bernstein's (1991) view is that the image can be built into a product, whereas it can at best only be adjusted for a company, while Macrae (1991) believes that a corporate brand can be translated into a mission of pride for staff in the pursuit of excellence, advancing company reputation among stakeholders. From this a branded corporate image can grow into reality.

With the derogatory representation of image as being artificial, the work of O'Sullivan *et al* (1994) was seminal in that it approached the subject of image in terms of its original meaning as being a visual representation of reality, which is important in understanding the world around us, whether employee or shareholder of a company. An interesting case in point is the British retail giant, Marks & Spencer plc, whose corporate image design had hardly become what Gorb called 'trivialized' and whose dynamics within the firm had more to do with manners and interrelationships than markets. Nevertheless, it currently has to rework its existing image if it is to evolve and adapt to meet its corporate values while meeting the expectations of its stakeholders, especially its customers who have deserted it.

Mackiewicz's definition of corporate image as 'the perceived sum of the entire organization, its plans and objectives' is very relevant to this case. By arguing that corporate image encompasses the company's products, services, management style, corporate communication and actions around the world, he could be describing any organization in crisis where the positive sum of these perceptual components must be re-evaluated to give the company back the market advantages it once enjoyed or to increase market share and investor popularity. A neutral corporate image can develop over time to become what Boorstin (1963) would describe as so impartial that it repels nobody. Indeed, Kotler (1988) suggests that corporate image can be highly specific or highly diffused and that some organizations may not want or need a very specific image. Some organizations prefer a diffused image so that different groups can project their needs into the organization, and this has clearly taken place in people's psyche, he implies.

Corporate identity

If there is a clear correlation between business policy and corporate image in terms of corporate strategy, perhaps the first question the strategist must ask is, 'Who do we think we are?' then, 'What is our identity and do we represent a clear business face to the world?' If an organization is unclear about its identity, then it will not be able to assess its image as perceived by the different stakeholders, nor how these perceptions should be prioritized in terms of strategic planning, policy and practice. For any business strategy to be effective, it must be comprehended accurately by the target publics, or at least in the way that the corporate vision and mission determine.

One area where image and identity overlap is in attempting to pinpoint how and when rumours start about an organization and how they circulate. Kimmel (2004) cites Koenig who believed that rumours are characterized by the four Cs: crisis, conflict, catastrophe and commerce. The in-house public relations strategist will always have the dubious task of alerting the main board to a rumour before evaluating it and acting on the communication or public relations strategy deemed essential for fighting it. A rumour control action plan can quickly be implemented with the internet and viral capacity, although while it may be important to be sure of one's facts, clearly there are circumstances in which it may be best not to respond at all. That decision may sometimes depend on the personality of the firm, as experienced through its advertising and PR promotional activity.

But how does a PR or communication expert perceive and project the personality of their company? The Corporate Reputation Institute (CRI) uses standard personality tests to compare companies with psychological profiles of people in an attempt to reveal and measure the emotional bond between corporate identity and stakeholder image of an organization. The CIPR has always stressed in its mission the positive nature of mutual understanding and goodwill, the relations part of 'public relations', but corporate personality theory suggests the importance of emotional elements in any relationship and often interpretive and cultural views. The traits of agreeableness, enterprise, competence, chic, ruthlessness, machismo and informality are defined by the CRI as seven dimensions of corporate personality. These are the factors that will impact on the ability to disseminate, evaluate and control efforts to scotch rumours, whether true or false, as soon as possible.

Visual identity

Whatever type of leader the CEO happens to be, he or she represents the cultural values of the organization and underpins the cultural web that emanates from his or her office. Cultural webs play an important part in understanding corporate identity; a visual identity step model might look something like that shown in Table 3.1.

Corporate visual identity supports reputation through the interrelated dimensions of visibility, distinctiveness, authenticity, transparency and

Table 3.1   *A visual identity step model*

Corporate identity	Objectives	Key issue	Methodology
Situation analysis	Analysing corporate expression and customer impressions	Determining perception of the firm's and competitors' aesthetic output	Corporate expressions/ customer impressions research
Designing the aesthetics strategy	Creating distinct impactive aesthetic impressions	Selecting strategically appropriate styles and themes	The styles and themes inventory
Building the collection of design elements	Implementing the strategy with rules of balance	Organizing and managing the implementation	The aesthetics balance sheet
Aesthetics quality control	Monitoring, tracking and adjusting corporate aesthetics over time	Evaluation of prior outputs in the framework and fine-tuning including updating	Aesthetics impact tracking

consistency, according to research by van den Bosch *et al* (2005). They assert that visual identity supports reputation through 'impressive design, effective application on a range of identity carriers and the condition of these carriers'.

Logos and livery: semiotics

In Europe, the science of signs was called 'semiology' and introduced in the 1990s by Swiss linguist, Ferdinand de Sanssure. In the United States, Charles Sanders Peirce developed the ideas and called it 'semiotics', which is the term generally used today to describe visual communication.

Three key principles underline the way we interpret meaning, namely the art form of the signs themselves, the way they are systemized and the context in which they appear. David Crow (2003) reminds us that Umberto Eco showed how the cultural background of the reader affects the way meaning is gauged from a sign to create individual perceptions and perspective. In his seminal text, *The Open Work* (1989), Eco helps to explain today's increasing dependence on visual language and iconic symbols at their most simplest, when he wrote 'the richest form of communication – richest because most open – ... a delicate balance permitting the nearest order within the maximum disorder'. This includes graffiti, or unofficial visual language by alternative communities, especially those who feel marginalized by a prevailing culture or officialdom.

The study of signs and symbols, especially the relations between written or spoken signs and their referents in the physical world or the world of ideas, is of increasing importance in the global marketplace (see Figure 2.8 on page 46). Awareness and respect for cultural similarities, differences and the value people place on logos and livery, is of pressing concern to marketeers and others who aim to influence customers and other stakeholders outside the home country. In a world of information overload, competition between brands at product and corporate level is fierce. In many instances, public relations budgets have had to prioritize rebranding by judicious and creative change in design and colour of logos and livery, both at product (micro) and organizational (macro) levels.

For the 2006 rebranding of Germany 'Land of Ideas – Time to Make Friends' campaign, the World War II images proved hard to shake off. Public relations research showed that young people no longer carried some of the 60-year burdens of guilt felt by their parents and grandparents, and loved the 'You are Germany' government advertising promotion for the five World Cup matches at Leipzig stadium. It promoted a new Deutschland with modern music, art, film, a woman from the East as Chancellor and a British-style multiculturalism (Channel 4 News, 1 April 2006).

In Germany, the research, monitoring and evaluation of image and identity were complex interactive psychological and behavioural activities. Messages must reach many different stakeholders on many different subjects while retaining a core image, even though those stakeholders' expectations are different. In making what O'Sullivan *et al* (1994) called the 'visual representation of reality', corporate image, based on clear identity, must be made tangible and quantifiable. Only then is it possible to realize competitive advantage.

Substance vs style

At the organizational level, Dowling (1993) suggested that in measuring corporate image and culture internally, the effects of mass communication achieved through advertising and corporate identity programmes and changing customer perceptions of the company by employees must be taken into account. If change is desired, rigorous control is essential. If the wrong variables are changed or the sequence of change is wrong, the result can be costly failure. A company's communication strategy tries to cover every aspect of an organization that its stakeholders are or should be aware of. Stanley (1991) argued that no organization can fool its stakeholders with hype. Corporate communication is only effective if it conveys a message of strength and substance based on sound and accepted corporate values and objectives, both internally and externally.

Stuart (1999) believes that corporate identity models, by including variables of organizational culture, corporate strategy, corporate communication and integrated communication, provide a more definitive model of a modern management process. In the era of global communications these corporate values have come to the fore. The internet has made debates on social responsibility and accountability a new type of challenge for corporate image campaigning. Ethical issues can arise from any part of an organization's business activity and thus form part of the core business operation.

There is hardly one aspect of public relations or corporate communication that can avoid addressing corporate identity, whether in terms of the letter of the law or the spirit of sound corporate citizenship. It is increasingly recognized that the value of ethics statements goes beyond the interest of employee stakeholder groups to embrace all other stakeholders, if not society as a whole, by adding value to an organization. Houlden (1988) recognized that being proactive about the way society views a company is a key skill for modern-day organizational leaders if corporate image is not to be damaged. Singer (1993) calls this 'consequentialism', meaning that ethical judgement goes beyond individual likes and dislikes to produce

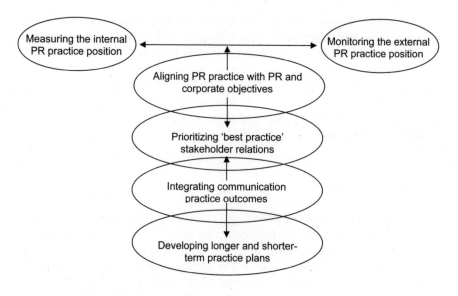

Figure 3.1 *PR operational strategy process*

social mores and norms that form the core of any corporate value system, no matter where or how a company operates.

Reputation indices

Nowhere has the issue of measurement methods in practice been more debated than in the area of US multinational companies and the reputations that they attract. The readers of the magazine *Fortune* are asked to rate the largest companies in their own commercial sector on eight key factors using a scale of 0–10 for quality of management; quality of products or services; financial soundness; ability to attract, develop and keep talented people; use of corporate assets; value as long-term investment; innovativeness; community and environmental responsibility.

This particular technique, called the *Fortune* Corporate Reputation Index, along with other measures such as the UK's *Financial Times/* PricewaterhouseCoopers seven-factor model of business performance, have been criticized by van Riel (1995). Drawing on the criticisms of Maathuis (1993) and Fryxell and Wang (1994), he argues that although these surveys are based on the opinions of so-called experts, 'it is likely that different results would be obtained were the same measurement instrument used by a different group'. Further, 'as a consequence, reputation scores as evaluated by the *Fortune* respondents relate more directly to reputation as a measure of an investment'.

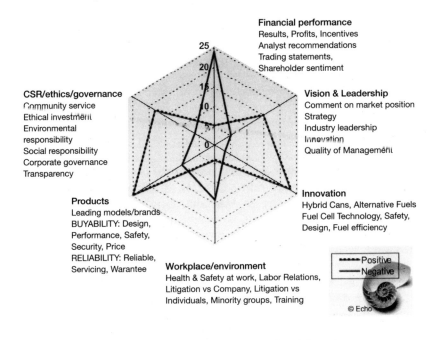

Corporate Reputation Drivers (Automotive Manufacturers)
by volume of Positive vs Negative comment

Figure 3.2 *Corporate reputation drivers*

Van Riel fails to make a positive correlation between the concepts of image, identity and reputation in measurable terms and even appears in places to use the words interchangeably. However, his work on applied image research and the various methods in frequent use warns practitioners that the quality of research is determined not only by the methods used but also by the quality of the questions formulated. The degree of detail in the question determines the degree of possible refinement in the answer, he argues, and states that, 'if a company requires further information about its reputation, then it must embark upon research in greater depth'. A typical approach is demonstrated in Figure 3.2, produced by Echo Research, global specialists in reputation audit and analysis.

This inevitably has implications for the selection of consultants, who in the main are seen to be more objective about assessing the reputation of an organization and therefore more usually given the research task. Ewing *et al* (1999) argued that research is more thorough if the consulting firm has no prior connection to the company and is totally unfamiliar to the client. In such instances the client is likely to get more people involved in the selection process. Also, consulting firms with international links are favoured not only by clients who have interests in overseas projects but also by those who participate in large domestic projects. 'Firms that have foreign partnerships are preferred over the local ones because they are deemed to have the international expertise to offer clients better services in the long run', they argue. Their study also reveals that reputation is not a measure of risk and that 'both factors are separate constructs altogether'.

Ewing *et al* found that if a company does not think or recognize that it has a problem, it will be suspicious of an outsider who tells it that it does have a problem and become more cautious of unsolicited advice. In today's climate of corporate accountability, no organization can afford to take such an arrogant or complacent view of communication nor fail to address its strategic public relations implications.

One contribution to more objective assessment is in the development of measurable social disclosure rating systems for corporate social responsibility (CSR) PR programming. In Australia, social performance indicators are standardized in a rating tool based on the Global Reporting Initiative (GRI), which helps to validate organizational accountability to that country and to society in general. The system includes scores for vision and strategy, governance structure and management systems, credibility, labour practices, human rights, social spending, product responsibility, plus other soft disclosure points such as social profile and social initiative. The ability to assess reputation statements using a tick box process not only helps ethical investors and shareholders, but may also avoid litigation in the future. Increasingly, the discovery process and due diligence will pay more attention to the accuracy or otherwise of PR statements during mergers, takeovers, buying or selling of businesses. Kneejerk responses to media speculation can raise unrealistic expectations and market overreaction, leading to short-term damage limitation exercises instead of reputation substantiation that forms the basis of longer-term PR strategic planning.

CAMPAIGN: THE ELECTROTECHNICAL UNIVERSITY 'LETI'

The campaign addressed the problem of social solitude of Russian WWII veterans and was conducted in every city for its veterans. Its focus was the importance of appreciating history to avoid mistakes, leading to armed conflicts. Leningrad (St Petersburg) became an example of courage during the 900-day Siege (1941–44). Its residents defended the city notwithstanding famine, frost, exhaustion. There are not many Siege survivors left in St Petersburg, and they are only remembered on the VE day by simple gifts, while heeding and seeking young people's attention and care.

Challenge vs opportunity

1. Social PR-project 'The Route of Memory' was conducted by non-governmental organization Student's Group 'ImPRession' targeting a specific social issue. Project was supported by The City Administration and leading Russian and international companies: JT International (JTI), Pentax, GUP Passazhiravtotrans, ITAR-TASS News Agency, NPO Mikhail Shemiakin's Fund, NPO Blockade (Siege) Museum.
2. Specific problems were: a) Siege survivors need not only material help, but also moral support, especially that of young people; b) commercial organizations don't offer any material help to Siege survivors because they don't realize the urgency of this problem.
3. Geographical area: St Petersburg, Russia.
4. Effectiveness criteria: a) degree of mutual participation of both Siege survivors and the young generation; b) decreasing the project's expense by attracting the resources of commercial organizations.

Research

Secondary research was conducted to identify and analyse previous projects designed to help and praise WWII veterans and Siege survivors that occurred from May 2004 to August 2006. Four previous campaigns led by large Russian and international companies, such as Medem, Aeroflot, Megafon and RI Novosit and analysed in depth were identified and several weaknesses were faced:

1. short-term character;
2. targeting at both Leningrad Siege survivors and WWII veterans, but we think Siege veterans need special attention in Russia;
3. involving passive participation of the war veterans, usually in the form of veterans receiving 'thank you' gifts;
4. not specifically involving young people;
5. under-funding by a single sponsoring organization, which makes actions local and less effective;
6. lack of creative actions. The only original project was 'Bind St George Order Ribbons', however it did not involve mutual activities of veterans and the young generation.

Leti then conducted original research by informally interviewing and then consulting on a regular basis with city administrators, historians, psychologists, business and community leaders.

Strategic plan

Programme's communications objectives

1. Goal: introducing to the city residents' minds the idea that 'St Petersburg is the city which remembers its heroes, feels grateful to them and cares for them'.
2. Sub-goals: i) establishing communication and positive relationships between veterans and youth; ii) changing the attitude of business community towards the problem and engaging it in projects.
3. Objectives: i) realization of the complex of events which would create a common space for communication of target groups; ii) engaging commercial organizations as partners, consolidation of their resources, enlarging the scale of the project, lowering its actual costs by more than 50 per cent.

Measurable criteria to determine the success

1. Quantity of:
   - representatives of target groups actively participating in the project;
   - representatives of target groups informed about the project;
   - events that took place according to the developed tactical approaches;
   - mass media mentioning the project.
2. Reducing the actual project cost by at least 50 per cent due to consolidation of partner's resources.
3. A positive change in relationships between veterans and youth.
4. Introducing the problem to the business community.
5. Facilitating communication among the target audiences and key publics.

Target audiences and PR messages

(See Table 3.2.) Global key message (slogan): 'Memory of everyone – in everyone's heart'.

Communications tactics

1. The main original mass event with the participation of all the target groups: veterans' stories (20 seconds) about a day of the WWII siege instead of usual advertising messages in city buses after each 'next stop' announcement. After that a young man would introduce the veteran and say words of gratitude. Public transport, chosen as

Table 3.2 *Target audiences and PR messages, 'Leti'*

Target audiences*	Demographics/ Psychographics	Key messages
Siege veterans	66–90 years of age, socially unprotected, presume that the young don't value them	St Petersburg is the city that remembers its heroes, is grateful to them and cares about them
Young people	16–25-years old, students, have general knowledge of the Siege	The Siege – it's about life, not death
Business community	Socially active companies	The Siege veterans need support
State authorities	The City administration	'The Route of Memory' is the city-wide project of social importance
NPOs	Veteran clubs/Funds	Student's social project aimed at solving survivor's problems
Mass media	News, social, political, professional	The means for translating messages

*Residents of St Petersburg

audio information carriers, is the main means of transportation of our primary target groups.

2. A series of supporting events; photographers' competition among students; personal interviews with veterans; social advertising; press conference and demonstration tour by a bus of 'The Route of Memory'.

3. After realization: interviews with participants, mass-media monitoring; press-clipping; follow-up actions.

Action taken to consult with management and secure its support for the campaign

We consulted with the representatives of the City Administration; historians; psychologists and members of professional community.

Operational strategy

The plan implementation

01-08-2006 – 31-08-2006	preparation for the project presentation (fundraising, media kits, media base).
06-09-2006	presentation for students on the international conference The Baltic PR Weekend 2006.
08-09-2006	presentation for veterans at the 'Siege Museum'.
08-09-2006 – 20-12-2006	preparation for the main event (interviews with veterans, studio audio-taping).
01-10-2006 – 10-01-2007	photographers' competition 'Leningrad-Hero-Petersburg' among students.
01-01-2007 – 31-01-2007	social advertising (40 city-formats, film on five video-panels).
18-01-2007	opening of the photo exhibition 'Memory of everyone – in everyone's heart'.
26-01-2007	start of audio-messaging in public transport; press tour by the bus of 'The Route of Memory'; press conference.
27-01-2007 – 01-03-2007	press-clipping, media monitoring, etc.

Description of any difficulties encountered and adjustments made to the plan

1. Low activity level of young people meant that more motivating factors had to be found.
2. Interviews with the veterans about Siege days were psychologically hard for both the veterans and those conducting the interviews.

Campaign outcomes

1. Factual: 103 audio-tracks placed onboard of about 300 buses on 23 bus routes of St Petersburg; more than 102 Siege-related students' photos exhibited in the city centre exhibition hall; 178 mentions in all types of mass media.
2. Informed: 400 students; about 300 Siege veterans; 21 commercial organizations.
3. Participated: 70 students, 43 Siege veterans, nine NPOs, City Administration; five commercial organizations; two media sponsors. Siege veterans have formed a positive attitude towards the project and

youth as a whole, demonstrated by positive remarks made for the media.

4. One main mass event and five supporting events were successfully held as planned. Communications were established between different social groups: photo exhibition and audio clips for public transport were produced by mutual efforts of students and veterans.

5. Actualization of the Siege theme for the St Petersburg business community, who actively participated in the project and provided it with the material resources. The actual cost of the project was reduced by 95 per cent, from $45,000 to $900.

6. The key message for the City Administration was successfully transmitted: the project got the resources for social advertising, also reduced the actual budget.

7. Professional acknowledgement: PROBA-IPRA GWA 2007.

The corporate identity was developed specially for the social PR project 'The Route of Memory'. The logo's main idea: the image of symbolically-rendered radio waves (original media, used in the project) and the use of the St George Ribbon's colours – one of the most valuable military decorations in Russia. It was designed by a student-volunteer of the project.

Only such honest beneficent projects can help to defeat hatred, hostility and aggression in our world! (Oleg Balikovski, blockade survivor)

Thank you for the great idea and the professional creative realization. We can trust these students the future of the profession PR. (Azarova, L V, The Head of PR department of St Petersburg Electrotechnical University: Leti)

The war and the Siege already became the historical past of modern young generation, therefore it is especially valuable the authors of the social project 'The Route of Memory' are students. (Zorin, G N, General Director, NPO Mikhail Shemiakin's Fund)

REFLECTION

Based on the information provided:

1. Explain the campaign's links between image and identity in raising the morale of thousands of Russian survivors.
2. Discuss the differences and similarities between corporate branding and product branding.
3. In what ways did corporate visual identity support the reputation of St Petersburg/Leningrad.
4. What role did semiotics play in the campaign's success?
5. How did Leti's campaign operational strategy improve its own PR performance while contributing to longer-term social investment?

4

INTERNAL COMMUNICATION AND PR: Employees as ambassadors

The flexibility required of workers, whether management or otherwise, has brought about a resurgence in the recognition of the central role of employee relations based on symmetrical communication for a participative management culture essential to a democratic organization.

Mayhem vs morale

The best 21st century 'learning organizations' value and capture the intellectual and imaginative resources often lying dormant in their workforces. Few HR models move from rhetoric or ideology to the reality of today's competitive workplace without the intervention of expert communicators. Earlier in the book, it was pointed out how necessary it is for an organization to ask itself what business it is in, so as to articulate its mission as a basis for strategic planning.

In-house public relations specialists need to ensure that they have enough authority and influence to ensure that strategic plans and policies work through from the CEO to individuals at all levels of the organization. The public relations director, working alongside the CEO and being fully

conversant with the organization's culture and value system, is able to identify any changes required to that system for the mission to be achieved. Having sight of the strategic plan, the public relations team assesses the implications of the plan for public relations structure, process and resources. An appraisal of the tools and techniques required to motivate staff, retain key skills and ensure competency for enhanced productivity, performance and commitment through newsletters, reward, skilfully targeted messages and other techniques, is a normal part of such assessment.

Privacy and confidentiality

The principal strategic HR theories, models, plans and policies are complementary to those of public relations. They often require senior public relations managers to work closely with senior HR managers, especially in areas such as employee relations, collective bargaining disputes and other legal affairs. For example, in Europe the individual has a basic right to control personal information about him or herself under 'rights' based EC legislation, but this does not necessarily resolve conflicts between individuals. The right 'to have' is not the right 'to demand', and individual rights can be overridden by public interest (UK Data Protection Act, 1998, Schedule 2 and 3). Other aspects of this legislation include confidentiality, a duty not to disclose personal information and duties in processing personal data, namely the collection, use and disclosure of personal data.

With the increase in virtual organizations and the imperative to link employees in distant parts of a global organization, the need to control from the centre requires sensitive and expert handling if it is not to corrupt the values upon which most organizations in the West rely. In cultural terms, the corporate communication system becomes part of the core corporate business strategy binding the organization together. Quality of relations between HR and public relations departments in such matters is clearly of strategic and operational significance in the auditing of organizational performance, both internally and externally.

Communication as a core competency

It is interesting to see how few academic texts on human resource strategy include communication as a key board-level competency. Strategic HR planning, policy making and practice tend to be discussed in relation to recruitment and selection, performance appraisal, assessment, compensation, training and development, succession and career profiling, job design and evaluation. These are cited as being essential support activities for

operationalizing corporate strategy, but HR frequently fails to identify the contribution of communication or the analytical resources necessary to cope with leadership and the demands of constant change. An experienced public relations practitioner could argue that this is why so many large-scale change programmes fail. The role of public relations in helping organizations to change and to sustain new behaviours is nearly always underestimated.

Many key competencies for integrated human resource management strategy parallel key areas in public relations such as:

- specialists from both areas need to share sound leadership through the application of a clear organizational mission;
- competent managing of people, skills, abilities and knowledge through the gathering of intellectual capital;
- monitoring and measuring information to ensure that work groups identify with and 'own' the information best suited to their function and accomplishment of the mission;
- maintenance of a culture that contributes to an open system in which people feel they are able to say what they feel if it is in the best interests of their responsibilities and can offer potential for growth and development.

Human resources and public relations departments together oil the wheels of successful employee change programmes.

Communicating change

Large-scale change to internal communication programmes must address short-term critical issues, which in turn must be faced and understood by all managers. At the same time, global and long-term business communication programmes, published as documents, must demonstrate sensitivity to the needs of individuals. Change programmes must create a realistic view of what can be achieved and not rely too heavily on raising expectations. They must offer opportunity for behavioural learning rather than representational learning; that is, change what people do rather than awareness alone through the use of new words and language. The tension between what people say and what people do is a standard evaluation measure. There has to be devolved accountability of managers at the sharp end to avoid top-heavy and exclusive project teams who drive programmes without consultation and often with inadequate research. Change programmes must be open to changing environmental pressures and priorities and take into account sensitivities that emerge from short-term pragmatists and long-term cynics who refuse to engage emotionally.

A 2006 dispute between London's underground train workers and management reflected a 1994 signal workers' dispute in British Rail. Crossman and McIlwee (1995) identified nine key motivating forces at such times, in which public relations clearly plays an important role. These are:

1. political forces;
2. economic forces;
3. cultural forces;
4. mission and strategy;
5. organization structure;
6. how human resources are managed in terms of flexibility, quality, commitment and strategic integration;
7. stakeholders' interests;
8. community relations;
9. union relations.

Much analysis in the human resource literature about the case fails to incorporate public relations criteria and so rarely offers resolution incorporating joint metrication.

Change development plans

All internal communication relies on basic principles of public relations, which include clearly defined stakeholders' groups, both formal and informal, plus appropriate channels for information delivery (one-way) and symmetrical communication (two-way). However, given that change is a permanent scenario in many organizations, communication managers need all the public relations skills at their disposal to ensure that staff contribute to decision making, ownership of the outcomes and subsequent supportive action for any change development plan.

This means astute monitoring of structure and process, ongoing training and development, and comparative tracking of stress, absenteeism and turnover. Internal communication is sometimes subjugated, as low priority, to human resources departments to the detriment of the staff and organization as a whole. Employee communication strategy is a specialist area within the overall function of public relations, responsible and accountable to the main board. At critical phases in the change process, the public relations/communication director will need to put together an action plan on the lines of the example shown in Figure 4.1.

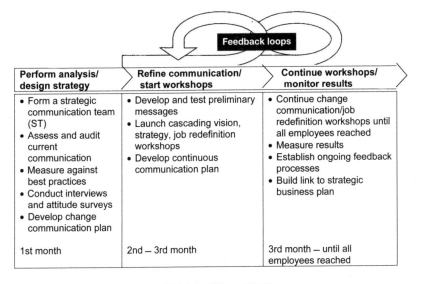

Perform analysis/ design strategy	Refine communication/ start workshops	Continue workshops/ monitor results
• Form a strategic communication team (ST) • Assess and audit current communication • Measure against best practices • Conduct interviews and attitude surveys • Develop change communication plan	• Develop and test preliminary messages • Launch cascading vision, strategy, job redefinition workshops • Develop continuous communication plan	• Continue change communication/job redefinition workshops until all employees reached • Measure results • Establish ongoing feedback processes • Build link to strategic business plan
1st month	2nd – 3rd month	3rd month – until all employees reached

Source: Adapted from Barrett (2004) in Oliver (2007)

Figure 4.1   *Three-phase communication change strategy*

Fairness vs flexibility

One of the first of eight data protection principles defines 'fairness' as collecting data only when provided. Data subjects should know who controls the data, what data will be collected, who will have access to it, and for what purposes it is being collected. It must be collected lawfully, which means complying with common law duties of confidentiality and complying with the Human Rights Act 1998, in which Article 8 concerns the 'right' to respect for private and family life, home and correspondence.

Perhaps the most familiar name to public relations specialists is Atkinson's 1984 'flexible firm' model. This UK model proposed that employers seek an optimal balance between functional, numerical and financial forms of flexibility by segmenting the labour force into core and peripheral groups. The corporate message must be consistent but may have to be transmitted in different ways to these different groups, whether they are performing in-house or as outsourced labour, such as associates or consultants.

Although the concept of permanent change took root fairly readily with writers such as Rosabeth Moss-Kanter, Barry Stein and Todd Jick, the proliferation of models that followed has sometimes assumed that all organizations are being affected by change to the same degree and in the same way because, among other things, of new technology. This is patently not the case, but clearly the larger the organization, the larger the change needed to alter character and performance, given organizational and decision making complexity.

A symbolic approach to decision making sees change as a process of developing myths, metaphors, rituals and ceremonies to cope with the uncertainty and ambiguity that planning and control measures cannot cover. It is important that the public relations planner is aware of which approach drives decision making in his or her organization if he or she is to articulate appropriately the meanings in the messages being put across. Whichever is the dominant force, communication is the essential leverage and link for any decision making, given that employees and managers will have participated in the decision-making process to ensure the change is 'owned' and can thus be successfully operationalized.

Another key area familiar to public relations consultants will be the concept of 'commitment', based on attitude, behaviour and exchange as a means of achieving flexibility and change. Exchange theory is seeing revitalized interest because it focuses on concepts of loyalty arising from mutual understanding and benefit. Organizations that demanded total commitment, often at the expense of work–life balance, family and social stability, have come under fire in the recent past and employers are now beginning to realize that there has to be beneficial exchange of one sort or another, material or otherwise, between both parties. Unlike economic exchange, social exchange involves unspecified obligations, the fulfilment of which depends on trust, because it cannot be enforced in the absence of a binding contract. Some organizations have therefore formally introduced the concept of the psychological contract as part of appraisal, whereby transactional contracts are linked to economic exchange but relational obligations or relational contracts are linked to social exchange. The public relations value-added component is measured by techniques that include levels of morale, performance and productivity, as well as traditional communication audits and suggestion schemes, employee rewards and recognition through awards gained by meeting sales targets and other objectives.

The organizational development movement of the 1970s focused on organizational change through the need to integrate systems and groups, including shared problem solving, which demanded higher levels of quality and leadership. The 1990s version of organizational development was about the dynamic links between business decisions, external forces and organizational consequences. It is here, in the concept of change and the lifelong learning organization, that public relations expertise is proving critical and high-profile once more in the 21st century.

Along with HR practitioners, public relations practitioners must promise or offer a way of linking the micro activities of individuals and groups to the macro issue of corporate objectives. So how and where do individual communication performance indicators link to strategic management?

There are three principal public relations processes that involve communication expertise and organizational behaviour:

1. quality assurance through communication audits;
2. expediting core values as manifested by the mission and ethics statements; and
3. managing new and more democratic systems of worker control through strong leadership and transparent consultation based on sound communication processes.

Communication as team effort

Strategic internal communication, as part of an overall public relations strategy, is a dynamic operational process linked to the business plan through some or all of the following professional activities. These should be carried out in conjunction with core human resource activities, probably in the following order, and prioritized according to circumstances:

- Establish and target formal and informal internal groups.
- Plan an integrated communication programme.
- Communicate effectively by word and deed through line management.
- Manage strategically around size, geography and international issues at home and overseas.
- Assess the competitive environment.
- Make every employee accountable through understanding of public relations and communication know-how.
- Decide the value and function of all publications.
- Establish fair and just employee communication channels, from induction to retirement or redundancy.
- Organize efficient monitoring and management of notice boards and electronic messaging.
- Maintain suggestion schemes through a rewarding open-communication culture.
- Incorporate crisis management techniques into headquarters record systems, computer networks and commonsense face-to-face briefings.
- Strengthen corporate identity and reputation by providing internal and external information.
- Clarify the relationship and boundaries between external and internal communication, the dual role and the capacity of those responsible to handle the delicate balance.
- Explain policy rules and regulations and be able to talk to people at all levels.

- Monitor attitude through communication audits.
- Evaluate corporate vision regularly with short-term aims.

It is outside the remit of this book to explain the basic concepts of inter-personal and group communication based on the psychology of perception and exchange of meaning. Suffice to say that internal communication as a core function of corporate strategy is no longer a simple question of effici-ent bottom-up or top-down communication via line management. It tries to involve as many people as possible in a common purpose. Intranet systems such as electronic house journals and newsletters help to make this possible, but never replace face-to-face communication between employee/manager and manager/director. This holds especially true in diverse workplaces where the potential for institutional racism, sexism and other forms of power play can be rife.

A strong and influential PR director, backed by a competent team, is the communication conduit for effectively facilitating symmetrical messaging to a CEO and main board for planning purposes. The director does this by managing barometers and collating and analysing intellectual capital that feeds critically into organizational decision making. Some of the difficulties for managers in attempting coordination and communication between many functional groups, units or departments are that they have their own professional ties to expertise and standards that may or may not parallel the objectives of the corporate mission. In-house public relations practitioners provide a forum for airing barriers to communication and provide the expertise in turning potential functional problems into positive contributions to the communication programme, which is fundamental to an organization's corporate strategy.

CAMPAIGN: AMERICAN AIRLINES, UNITED STATES

American, American Eagle and the AmericanConnection® airlines serve 250 cities in over 40 countries with, on average, more than 3,400 daily flights. American Airlines offers up to 37 daily non-stop departures from Europe to the United States. The combined network fleet numbers nearly 1,000 aircraft. American Airlines is a founding member of the oneworld® Alliance, which brings together some of the best and biggest names in the airline business, enabling them to offer their customers more services and benefits than any airline can provide on its own. Together, its members serve more than 700 destinations in over 140 countries and territories.

Challenge vs opportunity

As the world's largest airline, American Airlines faced a fuel bill as large as some smaller countries' gross national product. AMR, the parent company of American Airlines, spent US$6.7 billion on fuel in 2007 – up nearly two-and-a-half times its level in 2003, when fuel cost US$2.7 billion.

While American Airlines cannot control the price of fuel, it aggressively looks at every way it can cut costs that relate to fuel consumption. To this end, American created Fuel Smart, a fuel conservation programme aimed at engaging employees in these efforts. In 2007 the programme accounted for nearly US$204 million in savings.

The Weber Shandwick PR agency (WS) was tasked with developing a robust communications plan that consistently kept the Fuel Smart programme at the forefront of employee minds and reminded them that no matter the price of fuel, fuel conservation had to be ingrained in the company's culture.

Research

American conducted an employee survey on Fuel Smart and encouraged employees to participate by holding a drawing for a free gas gift card. The survey brought to light a matter that would have a profound impact on the way the team chose to communicate. The majority of the participants were employees at the company's headquarters or at its maintenance bases and had regular access to e-mail or the company's intranet. However, the Fuel Smart message was not consistently reaching field employees, such as pilots, gate agents, line mechanics or flight attendants who have limited access to e-mail or the intranet during their work day. A large mobile and remote workforce underscored the need to use a variety of communication methods to reach the largest audience possible. Instead of focusing solely on the Fuel Smart website as the primary medium, as in the previous year, the team decided to create a number of visuals and printed material, such as Fuel Smart newspaper, lanyards, banners, wallet cards and posters in addition to the digital media available through the company's e-mail and intranet system.

WS developed a communication plan based on the information compiled from the survey results. The plan was presented to the Fuel Smart team and to American's vice president of Technical Operations, Finance and Strategic Planning as well as the vice president of Corporate Communications.

Strategic plan

In 2005, the Fuel Smart programme resulted in savings of 84 million gallons of fuel, or approximately US$181 million, at 2005 fuel prices. For 2007, the programme's impact increased, accounting for almost 96 million gallons of fuel, or nearly US$204 million in savings at average prices for the year.

American's challenge was to keep the momentum going with current conservation efforts and to continue engaging employees to find innovative ways to conserve even more fuel in the programme's third year. It was important for American Airlines employees to understand that Fuel Smart is meant to be a lasting initiative, and not just the 'flavour of the month'.

For 2007, the Fuel Smart programme decided upon the following objectives:

- Reinforce the message about the ongoing industry-wide fuel crisis and its negative impact on the airline's business and operations.
- Inform employees of the company's progress and goals for 2007.
- Re-engage employees and targeted work groups in the solution by emphasizing what each can do to help conserve fuel.
- Inspire targeted work groups to more uniformly employ existing fuel conservation strategies.

Audience analysis

For the re-launch, American thought it was important to learn more about its internal audience for Fuel Smart, in order to build on the success of the programme the year before and find out the best ways to increase awareness and readership.

In the previously mentioned survey, results showed that 80.2 per cent of American Airlines employees were either very aware or somewhat aware of American's fuel conservation effort, and the survey also revealed an impressive 86.9 per cent of employees believed their jobs were directly related to the company's fuel conservation.

Operational strategy

- WS met with the lead communicators of eight key work groups to discuss current Fuel Smart communications and the work groups' communications tactics already in place. From this, WS formed plans for each work group, with suggestions for sharing Fuel Smart initiatives with employees.

- Leading up to the re-launch, WS met with American's Front Line Communicator (FLC) team twice. The purpose of these presentations was to introduce the re-launch to the FLC and to collect additional feedback.
- Based on research from American's environmental department, WS developed key 'green' messaging that showed the impact fuel conservation has on reducing the airline's carbon footprint. This messaging was weaved into all Fuel Smart stories and communication vehicles.
- WS worked to incorporate several Fuel Smart booths at employee fairs across the system. Employees were able to learn more about Fuel Smart initiatives and win gas cards based on their knowledge of American's fuel conservation programmes.
- WS created 6,750 'Key Action Cards' for six work groups to be worn with American employees' company badges. The cards had three department-specific fuel conservation suggestions and three 'fuel factoids'.
- WS distributed large Fuel Smart banners throughout the system to heighten awareness of the programme.
- Fuel Smart lanyards were created for specific work groups as an additional visual reminder of fuel conservation efforts.
- Fuel Smart posters highlighting conservation initiatives were designed by WS and supplied to American's hub airports to display in the crew stations and to maintenance bases.

In an effort to keep the Fuel Smart website's content fresh and continually increase interest, four new success stories have been written and posted since the re-launch and two new videos focusing on Fuel Smart efforts have been posted, as well as two broadcast clips of coverage on NBC Nightly News and the BBC.

Campaign outcomes

The Fuel Smart programme evaluated success in terms of fuel consumption reduction, as well as employee reach and response. As the programme continued, value and success grew every day. Results show the re-launch has been enormously successful:

- Fuel Smart saved 96 million gallons of fuel in 2007. At US$2.12 a gallon, American's average price of jet fuel in 2007, this was equal to nearly US$204 million.
- More than 12,000 hits were recorded on the Fuel Smart website in 2007.

- More than 500 employees sent ideas, questions and success stories to fuel.smart@aa.com, surpassing the rate of the previous year's participation by nearly 50 per cent.

REFLECTION

Based on the information provided:

1. Could American Airlines be described as a learning organization and if so why?
2. How does the theoretical three-phase change strategy described in the chapter compare with the approach taken by American Airlines?
3. Should communication with employees be the responsibility of an in-house human resource department, a public relations department or outsourced to a consultancy firm?
4. What evidence is there that the campaign applied teamwork as a best practice concept?
5. Does the evaluation indicate that short-term behavioural learning, as distinct from representational learning, has taken place in support of longer-term employee performance?

5

BEYOND 'CUSTOMER IS KING': Sales and marketing promotion

Relations between the marketing and public relations industries have had a chequered history in the past 20 years. Some would argue that they have been involved in a power struggle for longer than that.

In 1978, Kotler and Mindak wrote that there were four levels of public relations activity for marketing purposes, the first being for small, often charitable, organizations which, until recently, rarely outsourced professional public relations or marketing services. A second group, mainly from the public sector, do engage public relations services, while a third, small manufacturing companies, often use external marketing services or in-house sales personnel. Fourth, in large *Fortune 500* companies, public relations and marketing are usually separate departments, which may complement each other. In the past, they were coordinated by the chief public relations officer who would report to the CEO and the main board. Today's integrated communication strategies combine the managerial tactics of market research, advertising and public relations theory and practice, with coordination driven by a dominant coalition.

Conceptual authenticity

A current area of conflict emerging from empirical literature, case studies and the growing body of public relations knowledge as an academic discipline is that of the nature of public relations itself. No reputable profession can afford dissonance around its own identity or its public image, so next-generation public relations leaders and opinion formers must commit to a definitive acceptance of the facts of the 'nature' of the public relations industry as distinct from generally accepted notions about its 'nurture'.

There is a popular misconception that, just because approximately two-thirds of public relations agency fee income is used to sell product and only around one-third is going on government, investor/financial, corporate/reputation promotional campaigns, public relations is a simple communication support tool, albeit using a variety of tactical means, for bottom-line sales and turnover in the short term. Most large corporations and institutions now label their traditional public relations departments as 'corporate communication departments'. Whether the spend is on a corporate issue or product branding, it must be aligned to the strategic business plan in terms of time, motion and activity and be overseen by the board level corporate communicator/strategic public relations director.

In practice, many generic public relations operational tools and techniques support integrated marketing public relations activity. However, in theory, the body of knowledge required to forward plan and manage a public relations strategy is so aligned to corporate or organizational strategy that the reputation of the whole organization is more than the sum of its parts and certainly of any single product or service. This is not mere semantics or bureaucratic management speak. The history of public relations is littered with examples of the dangers of losing sight of core organizational goals or corporate objectives due to overzealous, creative marketing, especially during the 1980s/90s. That is not to say that profits from a single product promotion cannot sometimes bring about a healthy injection of much needed capital and income, eg iPod in 2004, but it does not, or should not throw the whole business strategy off course. Profits from one area of a business may be required to go into supporting other areas such as health and safety, technological and environmental developments in other activities, products and services at any given time. Better that the sales and marketing industry referred to 'marketing publicity' or 'market promotion' and dropped the term 'public relations' in its strategic planning and policy making.

The word 'relations' in the term 'public relations' can be used in a shallow or deeply meaningful way, and so the generic term 'public relations' should not be structured as a subsidiary component of a marketing function or applied loosely to the selling of material goods and services. This is not to take the ethical dimension to its furthest, ideological position whereby two-way, symmetrical communication is regarded as the democratic norm in the building of relations based on trust. In any organization, there are threatening or competitive situations in which asymmetrical communication is necessary because of received intelligence. However, as Alvin Toffler wrote some 35 years ago in his seminal work *Future Shock*, 'our first and most pressing need... a strategy for capturing control of change... diagnosis precedes cure' (p 430). He continued, 'we need a strong, new strategy... we can invent a form of planning more humane, more far-sighted and more democratic than any so far in use. In short, we can transcend technocracy' (p 400). There is a message here for marketing public relations professionals, as the following words suggest.

Today's wonderfully creative public relations campaigns that often capture society's hearts and minds must be underpinned by skilful diagnosis based on quality research so as not to intensify 'the rise of a potentially deadly mass irrationalism' (Toffler, 1970: 430). Whether through traditional methods such as advertising and events management, or modern methods involving new media and mobile telephones, Toffler's strategy for survival is ever more pertinent in our globalized economy. Unlike legal and social issues, commodities have shorter and shorter lifecycles in what Toffler called 'our high transience society' (p 67) and reminds us that 'in almost no major consumer goods category... is there a brand on top today which held that position ten years ago' (Schachte in Toffler, p 64) and 'in the volatile, pharmaceutical and electronic fields, the period is often as short as six months' (Theobold in Toffler, p 65).

Organizations are social institutions, whether operating for profit or not and, today it can still be argued, depend on:

> continuity, order and regularity in the environment. It is premised on some correlations between the pace and complexity of change and man's decisional capacities. By blindly stepping up the rate of change, the level of novelty and the extent of choice, we are thoughtlessly tampering with these environmental preconditions of rationality. (Toffler, 1970: 326)

Knowledge and skill

In the 1990s, a more substantive approach to developmental education and training emerged through the Chartered Institute of Public Relations for public relations professionals, the Institute of Advertising for advertising professionals, and the Chartered Institute of Marketing for marketing professionals.

In blue-chip companies, marketing, advertising and public relations functions are linked autonomously to the corporate and business plans but managed overall as corporate communication. Clearly each function is accountable for its own strategic analysis, segmentation and targeting of those stakeholders for whom it is accountable, but the overall organization's image or reputation must not be compromised by any one function. Of course, all three areas overlap at the boundary between themselves and at the interface between the organization and its environment, with consequences for environmental monitoring and research. It is here that the focus of each function must be independent of the other to maintain plurality of views and richness of information. However, the various perspectives must be brought together at a later stage for integration, then linked strategically with other functions such as HR, since environmental intelligence will have relevance for a range of internal functions.

Strategic planning for all functional areas incorporates analysis, monitoring of individual programme development, implementation control and evaluation. If there is a lack of control over any one area, say one attempting to dominate another for competitive budgeting or status purposes, then the communication strategy is put at risk. A climate of rivalry can be managed as a force for good or ill, depending on whether the culture is based on a closed or open management system.

As the amount of information flowing in and out of every organization increases, far exceeding any public relations strategist's requirements, the key task of any adequate intelligence system is to access and capture only relevant data and direct it to the required location for analysis by the right group at the right time. A focus on capturing and using pertinent marketing communication data, for example, will not necessarily help serve the needs of the advertising or public relations group as it may be too customer-specific at the expense of other stakeholders if not moderated by the communication strategist or overseer. Large firms have comprehensive management information systems, and the development of new technologies is increasingly making the selection and identification of critical data easier. Because of the need for longer-term relationships with customers, marketing professionals have been quick to realize the need for systematic design, collection, analysis and reporting of data. Findings relevant to the mutual understanding and sustaining of goodwill, traditionally seen as a customer relations activity, are increasingly coming under the auspices of public relations and referred to by marketers as 'relationship marketing'. This is especially the case in the retail industry, which promotes products and services through loyalty card schemes.

In terms of environmental scanning, market researchers analyse and categorize the economic environment in a number of ways. A common approach to strategic marketing is one where the philosophy implies that all organizations exist because they are offering some form of 'product' to someone else, whether it be direct, such as fast-moving consumer goods, a service offered through a third party and perhaps paid for by a third party (say, government), or a service in the community or to achieve a social objective.

Some of the rivalry referred to earlier between marketing and public relations departments in organizations has been about whether or not the principal stakeholder group or customer 'audience' ought to define the department's name. Traditionally, even though the communication tools and techniques available may be drawn on by all three functions of marketing, advertising and public relations, the dominant strategic force remains with public relations. The public relations function views its constituencies as consisting of a broader range of stakeholder groups or publics than customers, to include competitors and suppliers, employers/employees, community and local government, central government, financiers, investors and the media. Usually, only qualified public relations graduates are trained to appraise all ongoing stakeholder relations to ensure that the organization's strategic communication plan is coherent and consistent with the strategic business plan. However, increasingly, models such as the integrated marketing communication (IMC) mix model are emerging from marketing academics; see Figure 5.1.

Value-added

Of particular value to market research professionals has been the public relations evaluation concept of value-added, so the notion of IMC has established itself as a critical learning and teaching topic. Value-added is an accounting process that involves horizontal analysis of the industry a firm is in, along with a vertical study of the overall distribution chains to see where value can be improved and competitive advantage gained by strategic repositioning or sales reconfiguration.

Another important technique that overlaps with public relations is market segmentation. Guiltinan and Paul (1994) define market segmentation as 'the process of identifying groups of customers with highly similar buying needs and motives within the relevant market'. Segments are formed by identifying response differences between segments. They can be clearly described and reached, and are worthwhile as benefits to the organization. They are stable over time, so marketing programmes can fix costs to be acceptable. They will be classified using descriptive categories based on management's knowledge and experience of customer needs or desires supported by available information (customer group identification), or by the way customers respond. Groups can be identified by working backwards, for example noting characteristics such as the frequency of individual or group purchases or perceptions of brand preference.

Communication theory is grounded in models of perception from clinical psychology, a key factor in public relations academic modelling. Thus,

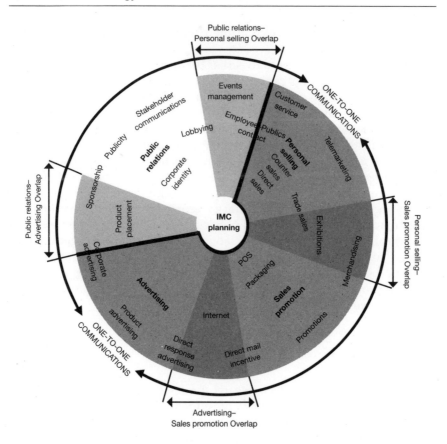

Source: Pickton and Broderick (2005)

Figure 5.1 *An integrated marketing communication (IMC) mix model*

another tool that is increasingly popular is the use of perceptual mapping, where consumer perceptions of product attributes can be analysed psychologically. On the two-dimensional perceptual map, consumers' reception is grouped together with competitive brands to demonstrate position and relationship.

Competitive advantage

Perhaps the most popular competitive advantage theory has been Porter's (1985) five competitive forces in determining industry profitability, which can clearly be adapted to organizational-level monitoring and evaluation through perceptual mapping and intelligence communication. Perceptual mapping is a technique that identifies gaps in the market to see if there is scope for a new product, or to plan branding or competing products in terms of particular characteristics such as price and quality. It is a useful concept for integrating marketing communication with corporate communication to ensure that publicity is coherent and consistent with the aims of corporate communication programmes, or 'on message' as the politicians say. Such analysis can produce public relations intelligence that feeds into the research, monitoring and evaluation information paradigm, as shown in Figure 5.2.

The importance of theoretical models such as Porter's lies in the focus on the competitor stakeholder group and the subgroups within it, such as rivalry between existing competitors, the threat of entry from new niche competitors, and the financial muscle of buyers and suppliers. The dynamic nature of competition and thus short- and longer-term relationship building is central to both marketing and public relations involvement, including lobbyists acting on behalf of both professions.

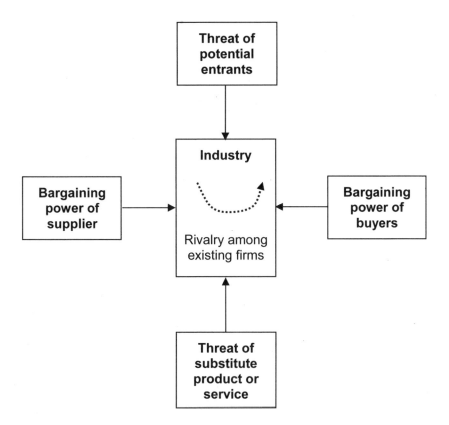

Figure 5.2   *Basic sales and market intelligence*

Increasingly, interest has been shown by the public relations industry in the notion that marketing tools and techniques can be applied to the competitive internal communication environment of an organization, because of the political nature of competition for jobs and status, thus creating a 'market' of the human resource function requiring public relations. Where once this was the domain of the public relations department, today it is sometimes thought that the marketing department is as likely to be aware of the corporate climate, structure and culture as other experts. Their knowledge and sensitivity to culture, orientation, power and influence will have been accrued from their analysis of customers, organizational structure linked to the marketing plan, and the interfunctional dynamics needed to operate that marketing plan.

Porter's theories of competitive advantage suggest that it is essential that organizations understand how the physical, human, financial and intangible aspects of an organization, including plant, equipment, people and finance, must be appraised together so as to quantify added value to the customer and thus to the organization as a whole.

The focus on data collection tends to be organized around customer databases, which provide insight into customers' behaviour and motivation in many markets, but particularly retail markets with data collated from loyalty card schemes in the grocery sector. One supermarket chain uses the Target Group Index, a research service that matches customer databases to three years of customers' buying behaviour; see Figure 5.3.

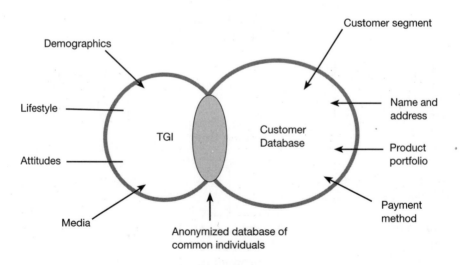

Source: Clive Humby BMRB/Dunn Humby Data Analysis Company, UK

Figure 5.3 *Target Group Index*

With the growth in service marketing and the development of relationship marketing, more and more organizations have adopted customer awareness programmes to harness the organization's effort to deliver improved value to its customers. This coincided with a general global economic recession which meant that, although traditional public relations departments had been removed or downsized, the need for public relations techniques remained. Market research departments found themselves on a fast learning curve to adopt the public relations skills and techniques required to cope with their sales and marketing strategies, given the rapid rise of consumer awareness and pressure groups. Customers not only had access to IT and media, but were now well organized and increasingly vociferous in their demands for value for money. If a particular product or brand attracted bad publicity, this could impact on corporate image, identity or reputation to the extent that the overall public relations strategy could be undermined, not least in respect of shareholder investment.

From the point of view of the overall planning process, stakeholder communication must be integrated around core corporate values, objectified by the production of mission statements. Representing the vision of what the organization is or hopes to become, the PRO collates the communication aims and objectives of each function, assesses compatibility and integrates them with the corporate business plan.

Customer relations

Porter's model suggests that there are three fundamental ways in which firms achieve sustainable competitive advantage through customer relations: cost leadership strategy, differentiation strategy and focus strategy. The difference between strategic marketing that seeks to interpret the organization's generic strategies into market-based strategies centring on perceived added value is that it is dominated by price. Other writers such as Grunig and Repper (1992) believed that the interdependence of stakeholder groups in the achievement of organizational objectives reaffirms the strategic role of public relations in the goals encapsulated by a mission statement. Marketing and sales management therefore would report to PR management at functional level, but directors from each department would liaise with each other at board level. Competition for budget resources between marketing and public relations can be ruthless. In-house self-interest, as the recent global banking crisis demonstrated, can override corporate loyalty and personal integrity where money and status are concerned. Cooperation depends largely on organizational culture and quality of leadership, as analysis of the credit crunch by the media revealed.

Because most sales and marketing becomes strategic at some point and because of the range of options available, the academic literature concentrates on issues of strategic choice, target market strategy, marketing strategies with demand, positioning strategies and marketing strategies for different environments. The strategy adopted will depend on whether the organization is a market leader with 45 per cent market share, a market challenger with 30 per cent market share, a market follower with 20 per cent market share or a market niche with 10 per cent of the market share (Kotler, 1994). Intelligence data from each market share will drive any public relations imperative.

Other areas of promotional overlap with public relations are in the sales and marketing of fast-moving consumer goods, as previously mentioned, and business-to-business markets. Consumer markets are characterized by heavy advertising and promotion programmes targeted at key segments so as to build brands and speed up the process of innovation and new product development. They also seek strategic relationships and alternative channels of distribution such as direct marketing and selling via the internet.

Business-to-business relations

In business-to-business or industrial markets, relationship marketing is critical to success, with particular emphasis on conferences and trade shows. Kotler identified three types of strategic marketing in service industries, with the company, employees and customers being linked by internal marketing, external marketing and interactive marketing. With services marketing, the different attributes of the service are identified or organized to target customer value and to position the organization to obtain differential or competitive advantage.

A public relations service must be able to articulate and prioritize any or all attributes offered by the service or organization in order to target customer value and to position the organization for competitive customer advantage. In global markets, strategic sales and market decisions are based on international research and may include looking for similarities between segments in different countries with a combination of factor and cluster analysis to identify meaningful cross-national segments.

Web analysis and evaluation

This has driven the public relations industry to look for new ways of measuring the impact of messages across diverse cultures and in shorter time frames. With export marketing, products are usually sold from the domestic base. With international marketing, products and services are marketed across national borders and within foreign countries. With global marketing, coordination of the market strategy in multiple markets operates in the face of global competition. One of the principal strategic concerns in the latter case is the task of developing the global portfolio, which incorporates a very high level of involvement from sales and marketing and public relations departments in developing e-commerce and evaluating purchasing and promotional web pages as part of the strategic plan.

Eye-tracking – analysing the eye movements and point of gaze of subjects in a market research or public relations study – is now an accepted component in most studies involving visual presentations. The technology has advanced to the point where data can be analysed in real time for computer- or TV-generated images or rapidly analysed with video analysis tools when the subjects have viewed a live scene such as a shopping experience. In Figures 5.4 and 5.5, an evaluation of a *Financial Times* page shows where subjects looked and for how long.

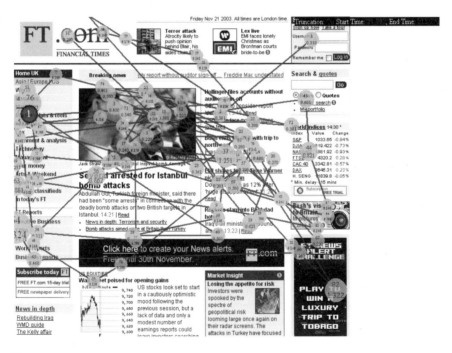

Key

Top left No 1 is the mouse click. The other numbers are the sequential numbering of fixations and duration while the lines between fixations represent the subject's scan paths.

Figure 5.4 *A two-dimensional view of a web analysis page*

Key

These are 'look zones', showing defined areas selected in the page and the percentage of time spent looking at them. The number 44 indicates time in seconds, while 42 per cent represents the percentage of time relative to the selected areas.

Figure 5.5   *A three-dimensional view of the same web analysis page*

Communication students generally understand the fundamental concepts of e-commerce technical infrastructure and applications. This includes electronic commerce and law, security and authentication, and internet protocols for knowledge-economy companies. These are key competencies for consultant practitioners who are expected to offer strategic corporate e-learning communication solutions for business and commerce. Furthermore, an understanding of the value/supply chain, with all its communication interfaces and the implications of an e-enabled supply chain, is essential to the marketing public relations practitioner. How people receive, interpret and respond to visual information now forms a critical component in market research and relationship evaluation.

Efficiency vs effectiveness

The effectiveness of any strategy depends in part on the quality of the monitoring and environment scanning within different environments, which are in a constant state of change. Of particular concern to the public relations practitioner is the problem of control. Not all marketing departments make clear strategy statements that are comprehensive or articulate the interdependence and interaction of the various elements so that the total mix is achieved in a harmonious way. Many a product promotion has created communication and public relations disasters when reactions to scandals became focused solely on customers and omitted to consider the knock-on effect of corporate image on other stakeholders.

Development of branding theory and public relations input into practice have reduced some of this difficulty, but at the same time have created semantic confusion when describing activities relating to both marketing and public relations. For example, Craven (1994) says that, 'a product is anything that is potentially valued by a target market for the benefits or satisfactions it provides, including objects, services, organization, places, people and ideas'. This description covers both tangible and intangible services and could conceivably include other identifiable stakeholders, beyond suppliers and customers.

Tools and techniques

Brand promotion, including corporate advertising, is a traditional public relations tool for adding value to a product so as to differentiate it from its competitors or to add value to the corporate identity. However, not all marketers see it this way, nor indeed do all other professional departments in the organization. Finance, for example, may be involved in designing pricing strategy, given, as Kotler (1994) says, that 'price is the only element in the marketing mix that produces revenue. The other elements produce costs'.

As with any policy making, planning and strategic development, evaluation and control are of paramount importance. A strategic review of marketing plans is usually conducted every two or three years to provide groundwork for long-term strategy development as well as interim analysis. It will usually consist of a full audit of the marketing environment and operations relating to all aspects of the corporate mission, objectives and strategies, as well as a review of the marketing objectives, strategies, programmes, implementation and management issues.

The role of advertising and publicity is to be cost-effective in creating awareness in the early stages of the product lifecycle, whereas sales promotion is used in the ordering and reordering stages of buyer readiness where the product is mature or in decline. Some of Kotler's views of the tools and characteristics of communication are shown in Table 5.1.

Christopher *et al* (1994) suggest that 'relationship marketing has as its concern the dual focus of getting and keeping customers'. They go on to develop a model that suggests there are five other markets that impact on

Table 5.1 *Tool characteristics*

Tools	Characteristics
Advertising	Public presentation, pervasive, amplified expressiveness; TV, radio, press, cinema, magazines, print, packaging, posters
Product/service publicity	Gain attention, provide information, inducement that gives value, invitation to engage in immediate action; competitions, premiums, gifts, trade shows, coupons, stamps
Direct marketing	Direct at consumer, customized, up to date; catalogues, mailings, telemarkets, electronic shopping
Press and media	High credibility, messages as news not advertising; press kits, seminars, annual reports, sponsorships, lobbying
Customer relations (sales)	Personal confrontation, cultivates relationships, encourages response; presentations, incentives, samples, trade shows
Marketing PR	Product pre-launch by preparing the marketplace for introduction of a new product

Source: Adapted from Kotler (1994)

the customer market: referral, internal, supplier, employee recruitment, and influence markets, and if marketing people are to tinker with all these particular audiences, the role of the strategic specialist becomes imperative. It is apparent that marketing models are linking segmentation to discrete variables within the stakeholder model. Meanwhile, customer communication relies on the traditional bottom-line approach (marketing) and the value-added approach (public relations), as shown in Table 5.2.

As with public relations and advertising campaigns, reviews are essential in examining the extent to which sales programmes are appropriately directed and whether or not a particular programme has been properly integrated within the PR strategy as a whole. This may include a product promotion review, where benchmarking takes place against external examples of best practice, which also involves ethical and social responsibility criteria. Some of the performance criteria and measures used by marketing functions are sales analysis, market share analysis, sales to expense ratios,

Table 5.2 *Towards integration*

Bottom-line approach Transaction marketing	Value-added approach Relationship marketing
Focus on single sale	Focus on customer retention
Orientation on product features	Orientation on product benefits
Short timescale	Long timescale
Little emphasis on customer service	High customer service emphasis
Limited customer commitment	High customer commitment
Moderate customer contact	High customer contact
Quality concern of production	Quality concern of all

Source: Christopher *et al* (1994)

financial analysis and profitability analysis. This is a costly process, and the results will be compared with various internal budgets, targets and performance measures set by the organization.

It is at this point that any positive or negative performance gaps, new opportunities or threats may require corrective action to bring the annual plan or longer-term strategy back in line with objectives. The requirement is often to identify the difference between problems, symptoms and causes that cannot be ignored from seasonal or short-term variations.

Third-party public relations consultants are often bought in, in conjunction with other management consultants. Where, for instance, some inter-functional relationship problems experienced by marketing and manufacturing departments cannot be managed effectively, consultants can provide an objective solution. Typical problems that emerge are products that have developed around technological capability, not market needs; products failing commercially; products being technically superior but priced too high; and concentration on tangible attributes superseding the customer benefits. Indeed, some organizations have placed research and development and marketing under one authority, in physical close proximity, or set up coordination teams or task groups on particular projects. The role of public relations may be to advise on internal or external communication processes, including impacts on corporate identity.

Marketing vs manufacturing

Other areas of inter-functional conflict may arise from:

- marketing who want more capacity, versus manufacturing who want accurate sales forecasts;

- marketing who want faster response, versus manufacturing who want consistent production;
- marketing who want sufficient stocks, versus manufacturing who want cost control;
- marketing who want quality assurance, whereas manufacturing have products that are difficult to make;
- marketing who want variety, whereas manufacturing want economical runs;
- marketing who want low prices and high service, whereas manufacturing often have high costs with extra services; and
- marketing always looking for new products, whereas manufacturing see extra design and tooling costs.

Effective communication between departmental heads is crucial, although few will realize that they are involved in public relations.

So what we have seen at a strategic level is the need for integration of all elements of the communication mix while, at a tactical level, some of the tools employed when implementing and evaluating programmes are now shared with public relations experts. As Smith and O'Neill (1997) said:

> Marketing used to be simple. So simple, it could even be left to marketing managers, but it isn't like that any more. The business of marketing, namely creating value by managing customer relationships, must be central to corporate management and financial planning. Marketing must be seamlessly woven into every function of those companies intent on getting to the future first.

More than 10 years on, market forces and economic realities have driven the commercial marketing, advertising and public relations sectors to appreciate how each of them contributes to corporate strategy in their own ways, both technically and tactically.

CAMPAIGN: HITACHI GST, JAPAN

Hitachi Global Storage Technologies (GST) was founded in 2003 and formed as a result of the strategic combination of IBM and Hitachi's storage technology businesses. Storage is one of Hitachi's five core businesses; substantial technology and financial resources have been committed to ensure a successful and profitable business. The company's vision is to enable users to fully engage in the digital lifestyle by providing access to large amounts of storage capacity in formats suitable for the office, on the road and in the home. Hitachi GST is positioned to immediately advance the role of hard disk drives beyond traditional computing environments to consumer electronics and other emerging applications.

The company will extend the world-renowned R&D heritage of its founders and build on their combined 80 years of hard disk drive expertise. With substantial and dedicated research and development investments, Hitachi GST is positioned to inspire and lead the future of storage technologies.

Hitachi brings a customer-focused and full-service approach to solutions for the hard disk drive market. The company defines the standard for product and service excellence with world-class operations, substantial technical knowledge and a comprehensive customer support infrastructure.

Challenge vs opportunity

Hitachi GST, the third largest hard drive manufacturer in the world, offered a new desktop hard drive that would be faster, cheaper and have more capacity than any other hard drive available.

Its PR agency Weber Shandwick (WS) faced two challenges. The first was simply getting people excited about a hard drive that would hold the equivalent of 1,000 gigabytes. However, it was still just a metal rectangular box that sits in a computer and records/retrieves data on command. After speaking with a few key journalists, the team's suspicions were confirmed – it would be difficult to interest them in hard drives, let alone hold their interest.

Research

To get journalists excited about Hitachi's new drive, WS decided to 'de-tech-ify' the product. To do that, the team researched the size and types of files people typically store on their hard drive and put together a terabyte 'Did You Know' fact sheet. The fact sheet included data such as: A terabyte will hold:

56 million 8½ × 11 pages of text;
1 million eBooks;
333,000 high-resolution digital photos;
250,000 MP3 songs – that's almost two years of music without hearing the same song twice;
500 standard definition Hollywood-length movies.

Strategic plan

Once the account manager had all the facts in line, an e-mail pitch was created and then sent to everyone on the targeted media list.

However, a major hurdle had to be overcome. The news of this new drive was extremely sensitive. Any leak could jeopardize the entire launch. WS was greatly restricted about what it could say. In short, the team could only say that Hitachi GST was going to be making a new product announcement on 5 January. Of course this 'vague' approach would net no media interest whatsoever, so the team devised their next course of action. They put their own credibility on the line. The idea was to tell reporters, 'Normally, I wouldn't press so hard for an executive pre-brief on this news, but I think you'll really be interested in what Hitachi GST is announcing. It's going to be big. And if I'm wrong, I would understand if you never took another call from me again.'

Operational strategy

With the planned approach underway, reporters started to suspect that perhaps Hitachi GST really did have some big news to announce. Indeed, WS lined up so many pre-briefs that the client started to get worried. 'What are you telling these guys?' she asked. 'I hope we're not over-promising on the news.' It was thought that all the pre-briefs went over without a hitch, but one online reporter who had been briefed (and who had agreed to the embargo), called Seagate – Hitachi's biggest competitor – and essentially gave away the story. On 4 January, upon learning that Hitachi GST was planning to make its terabyte announcement on 5 January, Seagate started calling all of its technology reporters and informed them that they would be announcing the world's first terabyte drive a mere 12 hours before Hitachi's news would cross the wire. While a few online publications picked up the story, everyone WS pre-briefed (except for the online reporter who broke the embargo) maintained their integrity and did not report the Seagate news.

With the launch of the terabyte three months behind them, the team embarked on the second phase of the campaign – the reviews programme. For Hitachi GST to maintain launch momentum, it was imperative to get out review units as soon as humanly possible. WS actually persuaded Hitachi GST to shift the first products off the assembly line from its internal sales team to WS. For the next five months, the team focused on getting a terabyte drive into the hands of every hard drive reviewer in North America and, out of the 40 tech publications the team reached out to, not one declined a review unit.

Three quarters into the year, WS knew the terabyte news story was old news and every publication that reviews hard drives had already published its reviews of the drive. To go after the same targets again WS needed to do something else. WS would suggest to the 100 top technology reporters in North America that they include Hitachi GST in any 'technology year-in-review' stories they were planning to work on.

Campaign outcomes

At the product launch, the team's metrics had been to secure seven prebriefs with 10 tech trade publication hits and one business publication hit. The team actually secured 28 pre-briefs with 23 trade reporters and five business reporters.

Coverage appeared in several hundred top-tier newspapers, trade publications, radio, TV, CES dailies and blogs, including The Associated Press, eWeek, Reuters, *Information Week*, *The Wall Street Journal*, *InfoWorld*, Bloomberg, IDG News Service, *Barron's*, *The New York Times*, *San Francisco Chronicle*, *San Jose Mercury News*, *Financial Times*, *PC World*, *PC Magazine*, CNET, *EE Times*, *Maximum PC*, *CPU*, *Computer Shopper* and *Popular Mechanics*.

At the start of the reviews programme the team's objective was to facilitate 10 product reviews and deliver three award wins. By the end, the team had placed over 40 positive reviews and secured more than 25 industry awards including: *PC World's* Top 100 Products, *PC Magazine's* Editor's Choice Award, *EDN's* Hot 100 Products of 2007, *Maximum PC's* Kick Ass Award and *Popular Mechanics'* Editor's Choice Award.

The objective for the year-end awards campaign was to secure 15 tier-one media hits. To date the team secured seven with placements in *Time's* Best Inventions of 2007, *Maximum PC's* Best of 2007 List, *CPU's* Holiday Gift Guide and *Computer Shopper's* Best List.

Finally, the team delivered over US$1.5 million in media value. Above all, Hitachi GST will always be known as the company that launched the world's first terabyte hard drive. On 5 January, Hitachi GST made history in what is now known as the 'Tera Era'. WS not only launched this revolutionary new product, but also executed a flawless year-long campaign that encompassed a product reviews programme and a year-end awards campaign.

REFLECTION

Based on the information provided:

1. Using the IMC model, identify which tactics have been applied in the Hitachi brand promotion.
2. How might the Target Group Index inform customer behaviour for future years?
3. What tangible significance would statistical website analysis have for the company?
4. How could brand promotion be sustained so as to add to brand equity over time?
5. How might communication be developed through strategic public relations to offer ongoing competitive advantage?

6

MEDIA RELATIONS: A borderless world view

Mass communication media have come to play a dominant role in the life of everyone, including the public relations practitioner. With the growth and convergence of global telecommunications and information technology, the role of these media can only become even more important. Few people, let alone organizations, dare to forecast where this will lead in years to come other than to suggest that the media will play a vital role in the survival of every organization.

Most large organizations employ agencies to monitor the media and to communicate with journalists, proprietors and other significant people in institutions who could be instrumental in the maintenance of an organization's corporate aims and objectives. Strategically, this role can be seen as a defensive, asymmetrical relationship or, in more enlightened far-seeing organizations, as a creative, symmetrical relationship, through which the organization can obtain the information necessary to be able to adapt to a changing environment.

Mass communication

The significance of mass communication media on an organization cannot be overestimated. McQuail (1994) ascribes five characteristics to the media that explain their importance to society as a whole, relevant to the modern organization at all stages of a public relations campaign or programme:

1. A power resource – this is highly relevant to organizations, given that the media are the primary means of transmission and source of information in society. A disgruntled shareholder wishing to unseat a member of the board will find it difficult to communicate with other shareholders in the face of the power that the organization's managers can rally.
2. As an arena of public affairs – for business organizations, this may seem less important than for governmental organizations, which are often the target of media attention, but many recent inter-company controversies involving government agencies have been played out in the arena of the media.
3. As definitions of social reality – at first sight, this is a nebulous concept and yet McQuail explains that the media are where the changing culture and values of society and groups are constructed, stored and visibly expressed. What society perceives to be the reality of organizations will be formed from a limited or non-existent personal impression gained from direct contact with the organization and from those images and impressions the media choose to present. Different sections of the media attempt to project different realities. For example, in the UK, the BBC 'Money Programme' presents a world in which it is normal for companies to compete with each other for profit without implying any criticism of the underlying capitalist principles involved. Left-wing publications will, on the other hand, portray a different version of reality, one that is much more critical and sceptical about the motives and social value of the leaders of major firms.
4. As a primary key to fame and celebrity status – this used not to be particularly important for business organizations. However, increasingly, leaders of organizations have used the media to project a desirable image. This is also true for authors of management texts who have become highly rewarded 'gurus' on the international lecture circuit.
5. As a benchmark for what is normal – this is particularly important for organizations where ethical issues are concerned. Currently, business organizations have to face up to the new norms of environmental targets, corporate social responsibility and other matters. Economic criteria used to take precedence over the views of fringe environmental groups, but the media now define normality as one in which an endangered environment must be protected and form part of the criteria for competent management. In the early 1990s, oil company Shell came to media attention over a proposed deep-sea disposal of the Brent Spar oil rig. Despite its eminently rational cost-benefit analysis, environmental issues were brought into the equation.

Along with these characteristics, academics are continually exercised about other qualitative variables in quantitative measures such as cost-benefit analysis. McQuail's two-dimensional framework for representing contrasting theoretical perspectives (media-centric vs society-centric, and culturalist vs materialist) is a helpful conceptual baseline from which to begin. It is shown in Figure 6.1.

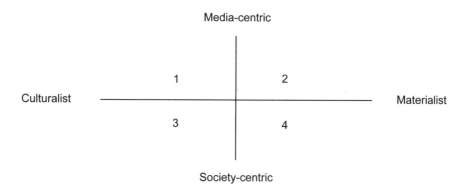

Source: McQuail (1994)

Figure 6.1 *Perspectives on media and society*

Rhetoric vs reality

Large organizations rely on mass communication, particularly in the form of advertising. In addition to informing the public about products and services and inducing them to buy, advertisements communicate messages about the nature of the organization and its values, which may or may not reflect objective reality. Ind (1997) believes that public relations activity fulfils a similar strategic role to advertising, 'in that its function is to increase awareness and improve favourability, but loses out to advertising in its controllability'. He uses as an example the American Anti-slavery Society, one of the longest and oldest public relations campaigns, which was formed in 1833 and established its own newspapers, held public meetings, distributed pamphlets and lobbied state legislatures and the US Congress demanding action to abolish slavery. 'Even after the American Civil War, the society still campaigned for constitutional amendments and civil rights laws to protect the gains of the newly freed slave. This led to the passing of the 13th Amendment abolishing slavery.'

The word 'mass' therefore can be given positive, negative or undifferentiated associations depending on the political perspective adopted. For example, positive in socialist rhetoric sees the masses as a source of strength, while negative, when associated with the dictators of the 1930s, subscribes to individualistic and elitist cultural values. However, in a communication context it refers to a large, seemingly undifferentiated audience. This is essentially an asymmetrical stance, because message receivers had little chance to share their perceptions with the mass of other message receivers up until the new technology allowed, for example, chat rooms on the web.

A note on copyright

CIPR's position on the current system governing copyright, information on the UK's Newspaper Licensing Agency's (NLA) fee structure for digital copying and general advice to follow when copying, covers paper copying, digital copying, intranet, and newspaper articles covered by the NLA. The NLA is a private company subject only to regulation under copyright legislation. Currently, all organizations copying material from national and regional newspapers (and selected foreign titles) for internal use are required by the NLA to pay for a licence. This includes the photocopying of press clippings for internal and client distribution. A list of publications covered by the NLA is available on its website. If a company or person copies (including digital reproductions) a clipping and distributes by fax or electronic means, they must also pay for a licence.

CIPR advises that the NLA scheme involves different licensing categories depending on the type of organization, such as standard business licence; PR consultancies, trade or professional association licence; partnership licence; or educational establishment licence. The Copyright Designs and Patents Act (1988) allows individuals to make a single copy of 'reasonable proportion', of a single article, from a particular issues of a newspaper for private study and research.

Message modelling

A pluralistic, process approach to any strategic public relations endeavour inevitably involves the mass media at some point. There are a number of different models that help to show how it might inform the public relations manager of today's organization. These include:

- The transmission model – this model views communication as transmitting a fixed amount of information. The sequence of sender–message–channel–receiver is now seen as naive and is replaced by the sequence of events and voices in society, channel/communicator role, message, receiver, thereby recognizing that the mass media are not the originators of the message, but rather that they are relaying their account of a selection of events.

- The ritual or expressive model – the former model implies that there is an instrumental motive in the communication process, that the message is trying to achieve something. However, communication is sometimes seen as a form of ritual when it expresses sharing, participation, association, fellowship and the possession of a common set of beliefs. Many advertising campaigns exploit the mass media in this way, not transmitting information about the product or service but rather associating it with a supposedly shared value. For example, a butter product might be associated with real ale as representing traditional images of rural life and the country inn.
- The publicity model – this sees the sender as not attempting to transmit anything, but rather simply seeking to catch visual or oral attention. The public may see the media not so much as a source of information but as escapism from everyday reality. Many organizations find it possible to exploit this aspect of the mass media, especially organizations such as Greenpeace, which can provide exciting and attention-grabbing film footage such as a motor boat cutting across the bows of a Japanese trawler, which guarantees media attention.
- The reception model – this argues that any meaningful message is built up with signs whose meanings depend on choices made by the sender or encoder. Receivers or decoders are not of course obliged to accept the messages sent. They can put their own interpretation on what they receive and therefore a reception model is dependent on an encoding and decoding process by those involved in sending or receiving communication.

All organizations plan their relationship with the media as part of their overall public relations policy. It is not possible to proceed without some comment about the term 'public relations' and the dilemma in which the Chartered Institute of Public Relations finds itself in terms of its own identity and reputation. Public relations has acquired a pejorative association in the minds of many people, being perceived as a process by which organizations attempt to conceal the truth about their activities behind a smokescreen. In political circles, a public relations practitioner has become a 'spin doctor' whose narrowly defined function is to deflect public criticism and to defend his or her masters or mistresses from public criticism. The shortened marketing acronym 'PR' for public relations is symbolic of this and, some argue, has added to the profession's status difficulties as it is often not regarded as a discipline based on reliable and valid empirical methodologies. Educators, therefore, usually avoid its use wherever possible.

Think global, act local

Some of the key issues affecting corporate strategy relate to globalization and new technology, which have brought about the development of worldwide networks, a widening of membership for pressure groups and a broader analysis of competition. It therefore seems an almost pointless exercise to plan strategically in a chaotic environment in which the notion of managing risk appears to be an oxymoron. If the power of individual nation states to control national economies has become limited, the problems of a borderless world become more acute.

As most public relations practitioners know, campaigns have to be planned at the global level, but acted out at the local level. The importance of regions or areas is defined by some degree of economic logic which may lie within a nation state or cross-nation state boundaries. So, just as the relevance of the nation state is being called into question, it is apparent that the modern multinational is continuing to lose what was left of its national character. Reich (1990) gave an example of Whirlpool, which employed 43,500 people around the world, most of them non-American, in 45 countries. He pointed out that Texas Instruments did most of its research and development, design and manufacturing in East Asia. Reich's research, although carried out some 20 years ago, still illustrates, if not more so, that a company's most important competitive assets, especially when competing in a global economy, are the skills and cumulative learning of its workforce.

Jolly (1996) wrote that, as evidence of a global public relations strategy, a company must be able to demonstrate selective contestability and global resources. Selective contestability is where the corporation can contest any market it chooses to compete in, but can be selective about where it wishes to compete. It is prepared to contest any market should the opportunity arise and is constantly on the global lookout. In the chapter covering marketing communication we saw that such organizations represent potential new entrants in all global markets.

Occasionally, the corporation may have to bring its entire worldwide resources to bear on a particular competitive situation it finds itself in. Customers know that they are dealing with a global player even if it is employing a local competitive formula. Thus global strategies are not standard product-type media strategies that assume that the world is a homogenous border-free marketplace. Nor are they just about global presence. If what the corporation does in one country has no relation to what it does in other countries, that is no different from dealing with local, domestic competitors. Finally, globalization is not just about large companies now that the internet makes it possible for small companies to trade worldwide.

Media transparency

International Public Relations Association (IPRA) members observe three codes – the IPRA code of professional conduct, the international code of ethics, and the charter on environmental communications. IPRA members expect editorial providers to observe the following:

1. Editorial. Editorial appears as a result of the editorial judgement of the journalists involved, and not as a result of any payment in cash or in kind, or barter by a third party. Editorial means print or electronic publication; radio, television, web or other transmission. Journalist means the person creating the editorial.
2. Identification. Editorial which appears as a result of a payment in cash or in kind, or barter by a third party will be clearly identified as advertising or a paid promotion.
3. Solicitation. There should be no suggestion by any journalist or members of staff of an editorial provider, that editorial can be obtained in any way other than through editorial merit.
4. Sampling. Third parties may provide samples or loans of products or services to journalists where it is necessary for such journalists to test, use, taste or sample the product or service in order to articulate an objective opinion about the product or service. The length of time required for sampling should be agreed in advance and all loaned products or services should be returned after sampling.
5. Policy statement. Editorial providers should prepare a policy statement regarding the receipt of gifts or discounted products and services from third parties by their journalists and other staff. Journalists and other staff should be required to read and sign acceptance of the policy. The policy should be available for public inspection.

Face-to-face or Facebook?

The full potential impact of the internet on media relations cannot yet be assessed, but there is clearly strategic potential for using it as an information and transaction channel, for distributing news and for building communication channels. Web pages need to be constantly updated, which requires investment in multimedia expertise. The design and research aspects of managing an organization's worldwide website are offering growth potential for many public relations agencies and consultancies, albeit their use is increasingly complex in terms of corporate communication planning. 'Think global (big), act local (small)' is no longer enough unless evaluation stands up to the rigour of quantitative and qualitative audits across barriers of culture, language, traditions and beliefs.

New research techniques such as web analysis using tools like new generation eye-trackers to collect objective data are changing the face of promotional planning via 'saved time', employing IT talent and offering new challenges to creativity. However, in the management of press and other public relations deadlines and the creative public relations talent that goes into campaigning, the ever-changing demands of media law should never be underestimated. European law on issues such as libel, copyright and intellectual property are critical to the underpinning of any public relations campaign or strategy. If an organization's reputation is to be protected, there must be respect for the spirit as well as the letter of the law. In the not too distant future, there is likely to emerge a rash of comprehensive and sophisticated books on the new technologies from mass communication specialists. PR practitioners should take heed.

It is thought that some 260 million texts are sent daily, but people are increasingly suffering from a sense of isolation where human interaction is substituted by technology. This is a recipe for confusion and misunderstanding in personal and professional lives because 'real life' through eye contact, verbal and non-verbal responses becomes displaced. To avoid online and offline dislocation, it is more important than ever to meet journalists and other stakeholders face-to-face to reduce the possibility of message distortion, whether delivering good or bad news.

CAMPAIGN: GLOBAL PEACE INDEX

Australian philanthropist Steve Killelea asked the UK arm of PR agency Edelman to launch his Global Peace Index (GPI) in 2007. The Index was the first ever survey to classify 121 nations by their peacefulness and had no prior media or public profile. On a limited budget, Edelman deployed a global media campaign that was the most covered news story on Google News on launch day.

In the first 24 hours the GPI reached hundreds of millions of viewers, listeners and readers in more than 100 countries and ignited a high-level global debate about peace.

Challenge vs opportunity

The challenges were wide-ranging:

- The principal challenge set by the client was to secure maximum high-profile global coverage for the Index and to spark a debate about the drivers of peace.
- Prior to the launch the GPI had no media or public profile.

- The GPI had to be disseminated on a tight budget to the media in 121 countries.
- Debates about peace are often controversial; Edelman had to encourage coverage that stimulated debate about the drivers for peace rather than the 'sexier' angle of high-profile countries at the bottom of the Index.
- It was critical to maintain the integrity of the Index as a pure piece of research and give it the voice it needed to help sustain it.
- There was a need to attract high profile patrons and supporters of the GPI.

Research

Edelman undertook research to understand the competitive landscape of other indices, the existing debate about peace in the media and the right calibre of endorser. Edelman analysed the media in all 121 countries to pinpoint a number of key target outlets per market.

Strategic plan

To meet the objectives it was necessary to engage, educate and excite both mainstream endorsers and the international media:

- Edelman engaged key UK and international media targets in a pre-briefing ahead of the launch to explain the complex methodology behind the extensive research.
- Edelman created bespoke media lists of top tier publications in each of the 121 countries and tailored press releases for each nation.
- Edelman advised that in addition to the main Index, there were 'regional' Indices to encourage comparison within geographies.
- Through the Edelman network potential supporters of the GPI were contacted and briefed on the Index and the campaign, which ultimately meant that the GPI was supported by Nobel Laureates such as the Dalai Lama and Archbishop Desmond Tutu, and Amnesty International Secretary General Irene Khan.

Operational strategy

The GPI was launched at the Foreign Press Association in London, attracting journalists from its extensive network of foreign correspondents, as well as UK media. The launch was chaired by former war correspondent Martin Bell and the findings were presented by Steve Killelea and Robin Bew, Editor and Chief Economist at the Economist Intelligence Unit.

Edelman negotiated an exclusive broadcast interview with BBC Radio 4's 'Today' programme. A central press office was also set up to handle media enquiries from around the world.

Campaign outcomes

Speaking about Edelman, Steve Killelea, philanthropist and founder of the Global Peace Index, said: 'I was impressed with the professionalism and dedication of so many people and their personal help and support through the process.'

- The Global Peace Index was the most covered news story on Google News on the day of the launch with 472,000 entries and an estimated final reach of hundreds of millions of people globally.
- More than a thousand global mainstream media hits in the first 24 hours; 1,500 articles achieved globally in the five days after the launch.
- Instant global coverage – in print, on air and online. Quality as well as quantity, with positive articles secured in worldwide media from *The Economist* to the *Sydney Morning Herald*.
- Sample of global media coverage: Associated Press, AFP, Bloomberg, Reuters, *The International Herald Tribune, Wall Street Journal*, Islamic Republic News Agency, Middle East Online, *China Post*, MTI Hungary, Focus News Bulgaria, Colombo Page Sri Lanka, ABC News NZ, Nartharnet News Lebanon, iAfrica.com, United Press International, The News Norway, The Peninsular Online Qatar, Pressir Jamaica, Pakistan Link, Poland.pl, *Melbourne Herald Sun*, IndiaeNews.com, *Malaysia Sun*, Zaman.com Turkey, *Middle East and North Africa Financial News – Jordan, Barents Observer – Russia*, Shanghai Daily. com, and *Portugal News*.
- Maximized broadcast reach through appearances on BBC World, BBC News 24, BBC Radio ('Today' programme, Radio 4 and 5 Live) BBC World Service (including South American, African and Asia sections) as well as CNN, Deutsche Welt, Al-Arabiya and One World TV.
- In the first three days after the launch the GPI was discussed on 350 blogs.
- Global Peace Index coverage and discussion continues months after the launch; New Zealand Prime Minister, Helen Clark and President John Agyekum Kufuor of Ghana have both referred to the Index in high-profile speeches in the months following the launch.
- Debate about the GPI still continues in top-tier media, and Edelman was appointed to launch the second Global Peace Index in 2008.

REFLECTION

Based on the information provided:

1. Which of McQuail's five media characteristics appear to be important to Edelman in respect of research activity?
2. Which media perspective did Edelman take when addressing the challenge of global peace?
3. Which of the four mass communication models described in the chapter broadly underpin the campaign and why?
4. Describe some of the issues and their potential consequences between the GPI and international media.
5. Describe some of the factors necessary to retain media confidence in the GPI through ongoing patronage and public support.

7

RESEARCH METHODS:
Measures and motives

Most management disciplines that are well regulated and well regarded are founded in established practices that are underpinned by rigorous research. Given that public relations is a management discipline, the lack of a reliable, generic research base in public relations has been a hindrance to the profession. For example, measuring the effects of core strategic public relations programmes over time as a value-added corporate component of an organization, whether in profit or not-for-profit enterprises, demands both pure and applied research skills.

The CIPR evaluation toolkit helps with PR programming and suggests a variety of useful metrics that can be applied, especially for media evaluation and integrated marketing communication. But the search continues for tools and techniques that offer value-added measures of return on investment (ROI). While there may be no universal method for PR performance, at least we can and should expect evidence-based PR linked to corporate aims and objectives. CIPR policy in this regard continues to evolve its evaluation agenda by monitoring and measuring societal, organizational, programme and best practice performance factors for updates to the evaluation toolkit. PR research generally emphasizes, like most business research, outputs and outcomes, but going forward, PR practitioners are slowly coming to accept the need for ROI tools where PR performance indicators can be measured separately from other corporate performance indicators. This requirement is likely to increase as metrication software becomes more widely available and which can be tailor-made to suit individual organizational needs.

It is not possible in a single chapter to offer a systematic exploration of all types of research and methods of evaluation, but some key concepts and approaches are described as an introduction to social science research as it relates to public relations theory and practice.

Art vs science

A more scientific approach to evaluation is emerging based on developments from media studies, market research and more specifically from both audience and social psychology research tools such as MRIs, eye-trackers and other high-tech developments. These provide essential information for the justification of public relations budgets through quality assured evaluation of strategic public relations programmes. The Dozier model shown in Figure 7.1 provides a conceptual matrix by which practitioners can classify and report the impact of their activities.

Evaluation and research also play an increasingly important role in the underpinning of strategic public relations systems and processes through the systematic gathering, recording and analysing of data relating to image,

| | Preparation | Content of evaluation | |
		Dissemination	Impact
Individualistic	Communication activities prepared via application of internalized professional standards of quality	Dissemination of messages evaluated by reactions of mass media professionals	Impact of PR activities evaluated via subjective qualitative 'sense' of publics' reactions
Scientific	Communication activities prepared via application of scientifically derived knowledge of publics	Dissemination of messages evaluated by quantified measures of media usage of messages	Impact of PR activities evaluated via objective, quantitative measure of publics' reactions

Source: Dozier, in Grunig (1992)

Figure 7.1 *Content and method in evaluation*

identity, reputation and perception by all stakeholders having an interest in the success or development of an organization. These include research into such elements as advertising effectiveness, media efficacy and corporate image, both internally and externally.

As the sources of information grow and become more easily accessible (government statistics, business directories, specialist digests and pocket books, international data, specialized trade periodicals, internet databases, etc), public relations decision making improves all the time. Added to this is the better quality of industrial and other surveys, including attitude surveys, field surveys and interview techniques.

In successful companies, systems are constantly changing and so executives' knowledge and daily contact with operations, the marketplace and consultancies create an ever-evolving strategy formulation process. At public relations conferences and meetings, workshops and committees, people from competing companies, suppliers and customers talk to each other and in this way often learn about the first signs of significant developments in the tools and techniques available.

The implementation of a communication strategy is often not thought out until the business strategy has been adopted by a main board or other senior management. Implementation is then sometimes left to the tactics people without clear guidelines, with the result that top-down approaches often ignore the contribution that public relations makes to competitive advantage in a knowledge economy.

At strategic level public relations affects the whole organization and so, inevitably, the involvement of all top management is crucial for success. At an operational or tactical level, awareness of public relations outcomes at the very least is crucial and needs to be coordinated and managed effectively, particularly at the point of decision making. Tactical communication decisions have to be seen to fit into corporate or business objectives and this requires corporate communication coordination and integration at board level.

Validity and reliability

Experienced practitioners are only too familiar with the dangers inherent in allowing style and creativity to run away with the substance of the original brief and its message, not least when a campaign takes on a life of its own outside the remit of the strategic plan. With the internet having driven general awareness of the importance of sound information as a means of influencing group management and their governance policies, the corporate communication industry finds itself revisiting post-war European precepts.

The global public relations industry has tended to rely until now on research developments from the United States and so most of the principles that Europe follows are deemed to be fairly universal, albeit with a clear caveat in terms of cultural similarities and differences alongside national and professional ethical protocols. This could change as the social sciences increasingly offer sophisticated methodologies because of new technology and software. Most practitioners are familiar with the advantages and disadvantages of internet-based research methods, not least in terms of environmental scanning or monitoring of media and other information sources.

In the 1960s, at the dawn of mass communication as we know it today, social scientists such as Otto Lerbinger and Albert J Sullivan (1965) published their now classic model of the four elements of communication: information, influence, impact and empathy. For many practitioners the internet is no different from collecting data by telephone, letter or fax, but it does facilitate the collection of data from larger groups of people and thus produce wider sampling. These secondary research methods are informal and can support formal research methods that require inferential reasoning, both quantitative and qualitative.

The most popular form of research into online communication is ethnography. Online discussion groups can reveal patterns of social relationships even though participation is taking place in a virtual space via chat rooms or video conferencing. Another use is gathering qualitative research via focus groups, and here the advantages and disadvantages compared to face-to-face, including personal interviewing, are about equal. The other key use is online social surveys by e-mail and web surveys, which can be used to supplement traditional questionnaires. This is the area attracting most government interest as a means by which democracy can be supplemented via the ballot box. Bryman (2004) identifies the critical differences between synchronous and asynchronous methods of data collection, the former being in real time, eg online in a chat room; the latter where there is an online time lag between the parties which is of unknown duration. This has critical implications for long-term public relations planning.

Some of the most interesting developments in online communication are the integrative approaches being taken by large organizations to teleworking, which concerns itself with both top-down measures of effectiveness and efficiency as well as bottom-up concerns for operational competencies. The implications for the public relations and communication industry are significant. Illegems and Verbeke (2004) demonstrated that broader strategic considerations, beyond the immediate impact on the bottom line, influence the decision to adopt teleworking or remote working, because teleworking requires setting clear performance objectives and measures to a sophisticated degree 'as business and society becomes increasingly IT capable' (p 333). Clearly 'the study of telework in multinational enterprises

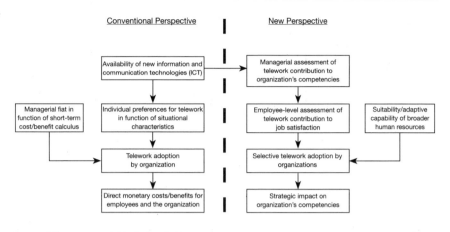

Source: Illegems and Verbeke (2004)

Figure 7.2   *Teleworking*

may be particularly important... to assess the impact of location and activity scope of affiliates within a single firm on the adoption of this practice' (p 332). Illegems and Verbeke cite AT&T, Signa, Eli Lilly, Hewlett Packard and Notel as just five of some 1,000 global companies adopting teleworking. Figure 7.2 offers two perspectives on teleworking that will influence future organizational communication strategies, especially employee and management communication.

Balanced scorecard

The balanced scorecard as a tool for in-house communication practitioners is only helpful in facilitating and controlling public relations performance measurements for management if it is applied as a strategy implementation tool and not just as a performance measurement system at particular moments in time. As Braam and Nijssen (2004) found when exploring the performance effects of using the balanced scorecard in Holland, 'mechanistic use without a clear link to corporate strategy will hinder performance and may even decrease it' (p 344) and that the way it is used is important when translated from strategy into action; see Figure 7.3.

However, at strategic and practice level an efficiently managed corporate communication scorecard supports coherence between conflicting goals of a company and helps to coordinate the various activities within the medium next to the PR goals. For example, media response analysis plays an important part in controlling multi-dimensional communication as well as helping to develop competent PR research.

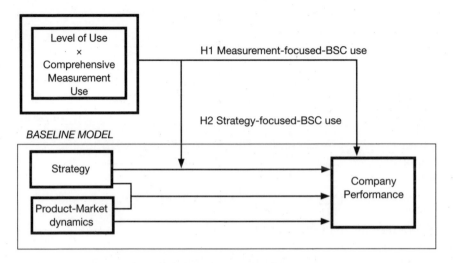

Source: Braam and Nijssen model, adapted from Kaplan and Norton (2001)

Figure 7.3   *Balanced scorecard application*

Scorecards are likely to increase in use because of the knowledge they produce as organizational performance indicators. One of the challenges associated with the use of scorecards is that they are unstructured and non-standardized and so must rely on expert linguistics and sensitive inter-pretation even when tailor-made for a company.

Use of the Corporate Communications Scorecard (CCS) by large comp-anies in Germany doubled during the last decade. A Leipzig professor, Ansgar Zerfass (2008), suggests five perspectives: financial, process, socio-political, potential and customer. These factors 'blend into the balance score-card of a company', he argues, without loss of the 'intrinsic tension between control and creativity'.

PR industry analysts

Perhaps the best informed about the design and application of the balanced scorecard as a strategic management tool are the industry analysts who gather data, news and information. Tailor-made analysis can be expensive and sound briefing is essential if managers are not to waste precious resources collating market data that is either too broad to be of value to the company, or whose accuracy is questionable. This is particularly true of service industries. The risks inherent in outsourcing this element of public relations management is probably no better nor worse than outsourcing

much PR campaign work to PR agencies, given the level of experience required in working with in-house management and their diverse internal
cultures. Strategy building may require non-disclosure agreements because
to do their job properly, analysts need in-depth information that is more
intrusive than, say, questions from journalists. In a typical public relations
department 30 years ago, the public relations director was the in-house
contact for both media and industry analysts. Today, with the acceleration
of technology, it is probably wiser to keep the roles separate so that everyone
channels requests for information through to an analyst relations manager
reporting to the director for press release or announcement approval
through the normal communication channels.

The main barriers to cost-benefit analysis measurement are cost, time,
lack of expertise and questionable value of results (Gaunt and Wright,
2008). The value-added components of non-financial company reporting
such as attitude and behaviour are well understood and public relations
practitioners with organizational psychology backgrounds are helping to
develop research methodologies for the public relations industry, with the
aim of moving away from simple input/output measures.

Grounded theory

Hence the current popularity of applying grounded theory for analysing
qualitative data. Academics still argue about a definition of grounded
theory, but broadly speaking, it concerns itself with the development of
theory out of data, with data collection and analysis proceeding in tandem,
consistently referring back to each other. This approach is called 'iterative'
or 'recursive'. It works through a process of coding, where data is broken
down into component parts and given names. It does not fit into pre-
conceived standardized codes, but emerges as the research progresses.
At different phases of grounded theory, the outcomes produce concepts,
categories, properties or attributes of a category, and hypotheses or intuitive
sensing about the relationships between concepts.

Computer software is helping to develop this methodology for qualitative data analysis in multi-culture scenarios. It seemingly offers a more
democratic way of creating knowledge through less rigid relationships
between researchers and participants. Such mixed research methods of
applying quantitative and qualitative techniques in the same project are
deemed to be more compatible with today's real world where information
can be misinterpreted or the cultural dynamics too complex to pin down.

With the speed of electronic communication, bad research can damage global
as well as local reputation overnight. For example, PricewaterhouseCoopers'
report (2006) showed that 'consumers and stakeholders do not understand

the drug development decision process in the pharmaceutical industry and do not understand the risks and costs involved in researching new drugs and bringing them to market'. The pharmaceutical industry now recognizes that drug companies must do more to ensure that clinical trial outcomes are reported accurately and completely.

PwC's perspective in terms of recommending PR actions essential to research and development and rebuilding trust (here, in the pharmaceuticals sector) is to:

1. Communicate to stakeholders the differences between chemical and biological innovation and educate stakeholders about the difficulties and nuances of fostering breakthrough medical products.
2. Address consumer misconceptions about the costs and risks of pharmaceutical product development.
3. Understand the most effective channels for the accurate and complete reporting of clinical trial outcomes by collaborating closely with health care workers and patient groups and establish links so information can be provided for relevant stakeholders.

In a democracy this means not only complying with the letter of the law, but complying with the spirit of the law in all activities, from the start of the research to its conclusion and public presentation.

Narrative methods

Many successful public relations programmes, including some of those to be found in this book, tell a story. Boje (2001) argues that a story is an account of incidents or events but, 'narrative comes after and adds plot and coherence to the storyline'. Philosophers such as Boje and postmodernists such as Jacques Derrida are exercised about the reliability and validity of analysis using story deconstruction. While the public relations industry recognizes the inevitable bias in any story rolled out in a public relations programme, it also recognizes that deconstructional analysis has a place in case study writing, the development of objectives, data collection, drafting a case, testing and revising. However, in the broader sense of public relations as public affairs, cultural considerations and ethical dilemmas, the following eight story deconstruction guidelines (Boje, 2001, adapted from Boje and Dennehy, 1993) can produce useful pointers to forward planning in terms of the acknowledgement of sensitivities and the identification of potential problems or issues ahead.

Deconstruction guidelines

1. Duality search. Make a list of any bipolar terms, any dichotomies that are used in the story. Include the term even if only one side is mentioned. For example, in male-centred and/or male-dominated organization stories, men are central and women are marginal others. One term mentioned implies its partner.
2. Reinterpret the hierarchy. A story is one interpretation or hierarchy of an event from one point of view. It usually has some form of hierarchical thinking in place. Explore and reinterpret the hierarchy (eg in duality terms how one dominates the other) so you can understand its grip.
3. Reveal voices. Deny the authority of the one voice. Narrative centres marginalize or exclude. To maintain a centre takes enormous energy. What voices are not being expressed in this story? Which voices are subordinate or hierarchical to other voices (eg, who speaks for the trees)?
4. Other side of the story. Stories always have two or more sides. What is the other side of the story (usually marginalized, under-represented, or even silent)? Reverse the story, by putting the bottom on top, the marginal in control, or the back stage up front. For example, reverse the male centre, by holding a spotlight on its excesses until it becomes a female centre in telling the other side; the point is not to replace one centre with another, but to show how each centre is in a constant state of change and disintegration.
5. Deny the plot. Stories have plots, scripts, scenarios, recipes and morals. Turn these around (move from romantic to tragic or comedic to ironic).
6. Find the exception. Stories contain rules, scripts, recipes and prescriptions. State each exception in a way that makes it extreme or absurd. Sometimes you have to break the rules to see the logic being scripted in the story.
7. Trace what is between the lines. Trace what is not said. Trace what is the writing on the wall. Fill in the blanks. Storytellers frequently use 'you know that part of the story'. Trace what you are filling in. With what alternative way could you fill it in (eg trace to the context, the back stage, the between, the intertext)?
8. Resituate. The point of doing 1 to 7 is to find a new perspective, one that resituates the story beyond its dualisms, excluded voices or singular viewpoint. The idea is to re-author the story so that the hierarchy is resituated and a new balance of views is attained. Re-story to remove the dualities and margins. In a resituated story there are no more centres. Re-story to script new actions.

Reading behaviour

Few people in the public relations industry believe that face-to-face contact with journalists and clients is obsolete because of technological developments like the new social networking facility Twitter. This micro blogging platform was used by Barack Obama to communicate with US voters during his 2008 election campaign and is used by top agency and corporate in-house departments as well as journalists. Like corporate blogs, Facebook and YouTube for marketing, Twitter is a new online channel of communication that is growing fast. With users sending updates in 104 characters or less, there are advantages, say, in crisis management but disadvantages, say, in the potential for misunderstanding. As more and more people follow each other with their updates and start to depend on social media, professional public relations practitioners must be aware that the benefits of using these new media tools will accrue only if the fundamentals of best practice are understood. The art and science of public relations strategy in the knowledge and expertise to be found in corporate communication literature and empirical PR research, is readily available to the thinking practitioner, but the gulf between knowing and doing can be wide.

This raises important learning issues, such as the difference between reading news and campaign messages in print and online, as well as issues about the use and abuse of the English language itself. Journalists and PR practitioners assume a lot about how people read news in print and online. The American Pointer Institute used eye tracking research techniques to test some assumptions by tracking readers' eye movements, comparing their reading behaviour and analysing the implications (see Figure 7.4). In what is possibly the largest eye tracking experiment ever undertaken, 582 reading session recordings yielded more than 102,000 eye stops or fixations. These were coded and analysed from the data set and eight key findings were produced:

1. Reading depth – participants read deep into stories in print and online, although reading decreases as story length increases.
2. Reading patterns appear to fall into two categories, namely methodical readers and scanners. Online readers were equally likely to be methodical as they were to be scanners. Print readers were more likely to be methodical, but both types read about the same amount of text.
3. Information recall – alternative story forms such as Q&As, FAQs, time lines, lists and fact boxes, help readers to remember facts presented to them.
4. Reading sequence – there was a key difference between print and online points of entry, with headlines and photos being the first visual stop for print readers, but navigation being the first stop for online readers.

5. Story packaging – lead stories and package stories attract more attention in print than other stories, where a lead story is one defined as having the largest headline on a page.
6. Voice and opinion – the voice of the paper such as editorials or celebrity journalists and columnists in broadsheet and tabloid newspapers generate less attention than might be expected, although print readers are clearly interested in the voice of the reader content. Letters to the editor and reader feedback are also categorized as voice of the reader.
7. Photographs and graphics – maps and explanatory graphics are viewed more than charts in print and online and as might be expected large photos and documentary photos draw more eyes than small photos and staged photos. 'Mug' shots receive relatively little attention including the pictures of columnists themselves.
8. Advertising – with broadsheet ads, a half page or almost full page attracts as much attention as full page ads. Colour advertisements in broadsheet newspapers generate more than twice the attention of a black and white one, but online, advertisements with moving elements attract more than a quarter of the total eye stops, with banner ads and small ads generating the most eye stops.

Michael Days, Editor of the *Philadelphia Daily News*, an EyeTrack07 research partner, says:

> I've read 80 inch stories that I could have read another 20 inches on and I've read 10 inch stories that were too long, so it all depends on… how was it done? What's the reporting? How's the writing? Is it a topic that really engages and captivates?

In a different setting and in collaboration with the Arts & Genomics Centre in Leiden, Netherlands artist Rune Peitersen also used eyetracking techniques to create a series of works to confront viewers with questions of what it means to see and be seen. The artist wanted to get an impression of what the eye receives in terms of overall position and speed by using a MobileEye, a tetherless eye tracking device consisting of two small cameras mounted on a pair of security glasses and a portable DV recorder. One camera records the eye while the other records the scene in front of the eye. The human eye moves constantly, several times a second, which we do not consciously control. These are called 'saccades', which are proving of considerable interest to psychologists and neurologists in terms of our understanding of perception, underpinning all human communication.

The relationship between newspapers and new media gets closer, with the internet increasingly taking classified advertising from newspapers and reporter bloggers rivalling opinion-makers. British journalist Andrew Sullivan nevertheless argues that although print media is in trouble, blogs are no substitute.

PRINT AND ONLINE MEASUREMENT

READING DEPTH
Participants read deep into stories (including jump text) in print and online, although reading decreased as story length increased.

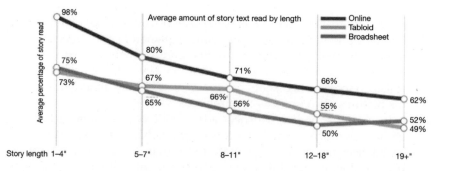

Key
Online participants read an average of 77 per cent of story text they chose to read. This is substantially higher than the amount of story text participants read in broadsheets and tabloids. Broadsheet participants read an average of 62 per cent of stories they selected. Tabloid participants read an average of 57 per cent.

Why would people read more of a story online? Home pages prominently feature brief, up-to-the-minute breaking news reports, which we coded as stories. We wondered whether the shortness of these and other online stories could have been a factor. However, when we looked at story lengths – from 1 to 4 inches for the shortest stories to those 19 inches and longer – we found that online readers still read more text regardless of the length.

We also measured whether a story was read from start to finish, and found 63 per cent of story text chosen by online participants was read to completion. Reading in the two print formats was considerably lower. Forty per cent of stories selected were read all the way through in broadsheets, 36 per cent in tabloids. On average, 68 per cent of the continued or jumped story selected by a tabloid reader was read. In broadsheet, that number was 59 per cent.

Source: The Poynter Institute (2008)

Figure 7.4   *Eyetracking the news – the Poynter study of print and online reading*

Source: The Poynter Institute (2008)

Figure 7.5   *A participant in the EyeTrack07 project*

Sullivan argues:

> the terrifying problem is that a one-man blog cannot begin to do the necessary labour-intensive, skilled reporting that a good newspaper sponsors and pioneers. A world in which reporting becomes even more minimal and opinion gets even more vacuous and unending is not a healthy one for a democracy.

Such comments lead the competent PR practitioner back to the issue of language and the English language in particular, as the world of business and commerce largely depends on it. American professor of linguistics, Roger W Shuy, argues for three levels of language consciousness. The first level is 'relatively automatic and unconscious' (2008: 3), the second is 'exemplified by those who write or speak publically such as... politicians or journalists' and the third level he calls 'the highest consciousness... evidenced by the fact that, in spite of the careful protection provided by executives and attorneys, corporations sometimes use language in ways that lead to business disputes, even law suits' (p 4). Thus PR practitioners face a new skills area, namely forensic linguistics, if they are to avoid litigation in an increasingly litigious global economy.

In a 1992 advertising dispute, Shuy (2008: 62) used 'linguistic research on narrative structure, morphology and semantics to illustrate how dictionary definitions are not always completely reliable and how electronic searches on language use can be helpful'. He applied Labov's analysis of narrative structure to the narrative part of a potential litigious advertisement and deconstructed it to show a six-part structure or portrait made up of abstract, orientation, action, evaluation, resolution and coda. Although the case never went to court, the company agreed to discontinue the advertisement. Shuy argues that there is a 'need for forensic linguists to be well trained in the sounds and grammar of various dialects of English and to be knowledgeable about available research in language variation' (p 150). The key areas he suggests are phonetics, morphology, syntax, semantics, pragmatics and speech acts, discourse analysis, historical language change and comprehensibility.

Although linguistics is an academic field in its own right, the in-house corporate public relations practitioner is well advised to seek the advice of the legal team when in doubt about global or local meaning. Alan Durant, a professor of communication in London, endorses the working relationship between linguistic experts and legal teams because of the way different interpretations can be made about everyday language as well as 'commercial transactions and negotiation'. He remarks on 'how easily it can become a minefield in social relationships... important issues not only about linguistic evidence in the court room, but about how contemporary public communication is best managed and regulated in a period of interpretive mistrust'.

Intertextuality analysis

Clearly, one area that is of particular significance to public relations practitioners is the way that press releases are written and designed to be read by different audiences. It is therefore useful to understand a little about intertextuality analysis so as to appreciate how each story is 'informed by other stories that the writer or reader has heard or read and their respective cultural contexts'. Boje (2001) believes that the narrative analysis of novels can be applied to organizational narratives as well, namely textual productivity, social and historical intertextual networks, intertextual distribution and consumption, intertextuality and carnival – what Boje describes as 'the theatrical resolve... to render various class, race, gender distinctions harmonious and therefore hegemonic with the commonsense legitimation of corporate texts, including strategy, identity and harmonious rationales' (p 76). Figure 7.6 shows historicity and social questions for intertextual analysis.

A key method of storytelling analysis out of the eight offered by Boje is theme analysis. Inductive theme analysis is popular among some public relations research agencies in their search for patterns, particularly of cultural meaning based on taxonomies of similarities and differences. For creatives in a global context, awareness of basic narrative themes is likely

Global social contexts

Whose social identities get constituted? Who has access to being included in the text? Who does the text quote? Who speaks for whom? What institutions commission the text?	Whose conventions (genres, styles and types) does the text incorporate? Who is the text distributed to for consumption? Who are the audiences this text is designed to be interpreted and read by?
How are parts of other texts incorporated into the text (quoted or interpreted)? How are various stories incorporated? What is the time and place of each utterance? What are the footprints of the author?	What is selected as newsworthy for target audiences? What are the 'common sense' or 'insider' terms? What are the parodies, ironies and metaphorization? What interpretative matrix does the author construct for readers to consume?

Precedent texts (left margin) / Anticipated texts (right margin)

Local contexts

Source: Boje (2001)

Figure 7.6 *Historicity and social questions for intertextual analysis*

to prove beneficial. In the taxonomy shown in Figure 7.7, four types of narrative are considered: bureaucratic, quest, chaos and postmodern.

Given that the sequence of public relations objectives will normally include informational, motivational and behavioural objectives (Stacks, 2002), narrative methods for communication and public relations research play an increasingly significant part in qualitative research.

In telling stories, an attempt is often being made to persuade through simple or straightforward explanation. With the popularization of science and technology, even generalizations must be based on clear, impartial evidence. Illustrations often contribute to clarity, with television and new media excelling in the speed at which they produce diagrams for news and current affairs programmes. Even when announcing a medical breakthrough or presenting topical issues such as nuclear energy, accuracy and clarity in reporting relies on the judicious use of language in its cultural context. Barrass (2002) reminds us that, although scientists and engineers are being asked to write well these days, many technical terms have additional meanings in everyday use and cites the words 'allergy', 'neurotic' and 'subliminal' as examples, with the reminder that scientific and technical evidence must ensure that such words are used 'in the restricted scientific sense' (p 59). Narrative methods must never deflect from consistency and predictability (reliability) or from validity, which challenges our perceptions both culturally and psychologically during the collection and measurement of data.

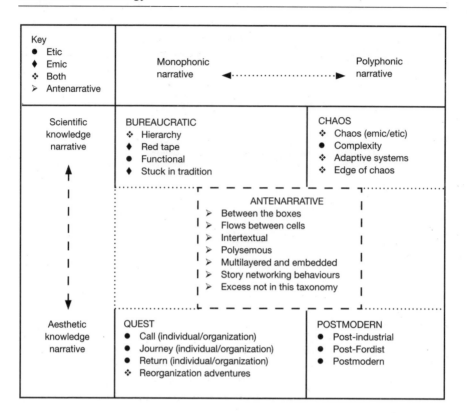

Source: Boje (2001)

Figure 7.7   *Basic narrative themes*

PR as a social science

The public relations and communication industry relies on inter-disciplinary and multidisciplinary research methodologies in the conduct of social research, including quantitative and qualitative theories, epistemology, ontology, the impact of values and the practical considerations of each factor. In a complex web, a crossover between market research and communication research can occur at any point in the choice of method, in the formulation of research design and data collection technique, in the implementation of data collection and in the analysis, interpretation and conclusions reached about that data.

   A stakeholder approach clarifies the boundaries in that the quantitative and qualitative research strategies for collecting marketing communication data will address issues specifically related to the needs of customers, suppliers and buyers/producers. This is true whether the research design is experimental, cross-sectional, longitudinal, comparative or a survey on a single case study. Even with the development of value-added public relations to the bottom line via integrated marketing communication models, the strategic elements are straightforward, particularly in respect of sampling – both probability sampling (random sampling) and non-probability sampling (non-random sampling). Although market-related public relations may appear to dominate financially in terms of fee income for consultants and agencies from consumer products compared to fee income to the public relations industry from corporate, environmental and governmental areas, the impact and often negative criticism of the industry is felt less because it has little or fewer social and political implications. This is particularly relevant when measuring public relations campaigns and communication programmes, such as surveys of levels of awareness or related attitudes, when measuring audience reception or measures associated with changes in behaviour, eg the behaviour of managers following an internal communication audit and corporate governance initiatives. The range of other stakeholders such as shareholders, educators, media opinion leaders, churches and state may be appropriate targets for the selling of a product or service but, in terms of public relations theory, selling is usually a one-way process (information) not a two-way process (communication).

Population classification systems may rely on research lists such as Mosaic, which is based on census data in the UK but also includes other data sources to produce a system of 11 groups, including Urban Intelligence and Rural Isolation. Other geo-demographic systems include The Acorn Consumer classification with five groups: wealthy achievers, urban prosperity, comfortably off, moderate means and hard pressed. These have been adapted to serve the classification needs of specific sectors such as investors and financial markets.

Theory can of course emerge from the collection and analysis of data, and qualitative research is often applied in the testing of theory ahead of data collection. However, multi-strategy research requires considerable research experience, skill and training and the ability to handle the outcomes, which can be planned or unplanned, qualitative or quantitative. Although this book is not a 'how to' book and so does not instruct the reader on how to carry out quantitative methodologies such as bivariate analysis, multivariate analysis or statistical significance methods, nor qualitative methods such as interviewing, surveys or participant observation, a chapter on research would be remiss without mentioning the software package, SPSS for Windows. This is the most widely used package for analysing data because it saves time and is fairly easy to learn. Most public relations postgraduate programmes include training in it, or if they don't they should do so, because experience of SPSS is necessary at research planning and public relations programme design stage, where it is particularly important for coding or labelling data or units of analysis and the coding frame in respect of the coding of open questions. In content analysis, coding schedules are produced as forms on which all the data about an item being coded is entered and preserved. There are statutory ethical governance and regulations on research that must be adhered to in the UK and which underpin the CIPR's code of conduct and ethical statements.

CAMPAIGN: ACCENTURE, GERMANY

Accenture's campaign pioneered the use of e-PR when, in 2007, the company launched a highly successful recruiting initiative in Austria, Germany and Switzerland (ASG). Based on scientific research, the integrated communication campaign made extensive use of up-to-date web 2.0-based marketing tactics that were supported by classic PR and advertising.

With this initiative, Accenture ASG exceeded its ambitious business objectives, detailed by predefined key performance indicators, but also achieved a positioning within Accenture's global group as a pioneer in web 2.0 recruiting.

Challenge vs opportunity

Accenture is a global management consulting, technology services and outsourcing company. With more than 175,000 people in 49 countries, the company generated net revenues of US$19.70 billion for the fiscal year ended 31 August 2007.

Each year, Accenture hires more than 1,000 people in the German-speaking markets, the majority of which are university graduates. The positions to be filled range from management and strategy consulting to the area of technology solutions.

In the light of the positive business development and the fierce competition for qualified employees, Accenture decided in spring 2007 to give additional impulse to its ongoing recruiting campaign *Ich bei Accenture* (Me at Accenture) through an intensive, temporary and integrated communication initiative.

Research

According to primary and secondary research, the special organizational culture at Accenture, which emphasizes cooperation, support and collegiality, was a crucial factor for the candidates to opt for Accenture, besides the hard facts such as interesting assignments and responsibility. In terms of channels, Accenture found that e-PR elements had to be an integral part to adequately reach its tech-savvy target group.

Strategic plan

The overall objective was to meet the recruiting objectives of the business year 2007 (01/09 – 31/08) and to fill the applications pipeline for 2007/08. The communication objective was to increase awareness of Accenture among graduates with a business, IT or sciences background as well as young professionals, and to increase the number of suitable candidates perceiving Accenture as an 'employer of choice'. The main target was to generate 5,000 additional applications in Germany, Austria and Switzerland.

The campaign particularly emphasized the human touch, authenticity and credibility, so specific employees were chosen to act as ambassadors of the organization in the search for new co-workers with key messages developed to communicate facts about work and careers at Accenture using an integrated approach via several channels involving top management.

Operational strategy

A microsite with up-to-date web 2.0 elements served as the central platform of the campaign. That platform was also linked to the permanent recruiting website. The core of the microsite consisted of interactive flash sequences that portrayed nine Accenture employees who talked about their jobs, their reasons for choosing Accenture as an employer, and their personal backgrounds. In doing so, every employee represented a specific job profile, the details of which were illustrated on a profile page. In addition, prospects could reach a blog (mit-macher.blogspot.com) via a link on the microsite, where Accenture employees regularly wrote about their jobs and answered questions concerning Accenture.

An integrated communication campaign consisting of public relations, advertising, events and viral marketing generated the required buzz for the microsite. Those measures started before the official launch of the microsite while the web address had already appeared in rankings of the search engines at the stage of going live. Three mood spots, short film trailers referring to the web address, were launched on YouTube and other video communities. The diffusion of the spot to potential candidates was achieved with the help of Accenture employees, who had been asked to support the campaign by management who had already introduced the campaign via a video podcast published on their intranet.

On the day of the microsite launch, a number of events took place in order to inform and involve employees at Accenture offices in Frankfurt, Vienna and Zurich. Two Polaroid photos were made of all employees when they arrived in the morning along with their web addresses. One photo of each employee was added to a collection on a pin board in the reception area; the other remained with the employee, in addition to a leaflet about the campaign. Furthermore, with their Polaroid in digital format, those employees were able to brand their profiles in social networks such as Xing.

After the launch of the microsite, Accenture started a campus promotions tour, visiting selected universities in Germany, Austria and Switzerland. The tour was accompanied by local media work in the universities' main catchment areas. In addition, the campaign was featured in career and human resources media, in the marketing press and in local newspapers and radio stations. Parallel with internal communication, events and media work, Accenture advertised in the relevant online media (eg Stepstone, F.A.Z Jobs, karriere.de, computerwoche.de, etc) as well as in the business press.

Campaign outcomes

The initiative exceeded Accenture's expectations and numerous pre-defined key performance indicators. In the period from 23/05/2007 to 03/10/2007, more than 82,000 users visited the microsite, and about 250,000 page views were registered. In total, the videos were seen almost 18,000 times. More than 2,000 search terms at Google generated more than 65 million ad impressions, which were clicked 62,000 times.

Accenture successfully presented itself to over 30 universities in Germany, Austria and Switzerland. About 240 Accenture employees were engaged in blogs and social networks, where they interacted personally with potential applicants and answered questions regarding different job profiles at Accenture. The most popular blog entries were read more than 500 times per week. The accompanying media work generated articles in the daily and trade press, as well as campus media and online publications, including *Computerwoche*, *VDI Nachrichten*, *Personalmagazin*, *w&v* and *BILD*.

Since the launch of the microsite on 16 May 2007, application numbers doubled. In June 2007 the number of applications was 250 per cent higher compared with the same month of the previous year, and by September 2007 the number was still 140 per cent above the number of applications received during the same period in 2006. The initiative not only attracted more people, but also the right candidates, and 90 per cent of all new employees at Accenture were aware of the campaign.

Accenture demonstrated its pioneering conceptional thinking regarding the recruitment of new employees. By effectively linking different marketing and PR instruments, including viral elements and up-to-date web 2.0 technologies, Accenture successfully involved its own employees, positioned Accenture Germany as a global pioneer and set an example for its other national affiliates.

REFLECTION

Based on the information provided:

1. Critically appraise the content and method of Accenture's evaluation through the classic Dozier 1992 model.
2. Given the criticality of the internet to business performance, what role, if any, might teleworking and balanced scorecards have played in the recruitment campaign?
3. In the application of key performance indicators, which of them proved most useful?
4. In the aftermath of the microsite launch, which psycho/social issues formed part of the integrated communication strategy?
5. If the core activity of any continuity planning is corporate communication, how could Accenture's university relations be sustained?

8

THE ETHICAL DIMENSION:
A moral imperative

Increasingly, communication experts and public relations practitioners find themselves involved in mediation, conflict resolution and relationship or personal communication development programmes. Christians and Traeber (1997) identified a broad-based ethical theory of communication that transcends cultures and the world of mass media. They believed it could be accepted by society as a whole and that organizations would find it possible to adopt and adapt it to form the basis of organizational codes. Christians and Traeber demonstrate that, 'certain ethical protonorms – above all truth telling, commitment to justice, freedom in solidarity and respect for human dignity – are validated as core values in communications in different cultures'. They conclude that, 'we are in search of the ultimate and unconditional characteristics of human life, from which the meaning of human actions can be derived. Communication is one such act'.

The development and pretesting of the means for achieving ethical objectives through research is one factor in the developing assessment framework suggested earlier in this book. Pretests are 'reliable estimates of how programme strategies will work', say Kirban and Jackson (1990). They warn of the danger of operating by instinct instead of employing creative and artistic decisions based on research. A generation ago, Ehling (1985) warned that public relations would be incomplete and flawed with technician behaviour replacing management-level functioning if it were not based on research. He believed that public relations is:

a decision-making, problem-solving activity essentially concerned with selecting and specifying end states (goals, objectives) to be attained by an organization or group and with developing, programming and implementing efficient and effective means (courses of action, strategies) for attaining or accomplishing the desired end states.

In 1978, the worldwide public relations industry produced the Mexican statement, emanating from an international meeting in the same year, stating that public relations is the art and social science of analysing trends, predicting their consequences, counselling organization leaders and implementing planned programmes of action that serve both the organization's and the public's interests. While key words in the original CIPR definition were 'planned', 'mutual' and 'publics', in the Mexican statement keywords are 'research', 'analysing', 'counselling' and 'both'. The Mexican definition excludes knee-jerk reactions to environmental influences and indicates that public relations involves an advisory function, which in any democracy requires a clear ethical stance. Public relations professionals, whether in-house or outsourced, give advice to senior managers in organizations and emphasize the need to serve the public interest, even where that term is ill-defined.

PR vs propaganda

It is essential to distinguish corporate public relations from propaganda, because public perception often confuses the two concepts. Elliott (1975) defines propaganda as:

> statements of policy or facts, usually of a political nature, the real purpose of which is different from their apparent purpose. In this sense propaganda existed before the twentieth century, but its importance has increased in an age when communication is easier and when it is more useful to influence ordinary people. The term is used to describe a statement which is believed to be insincere or untrue, and designed to impress the public rather than to reach the truth or to bring about a genuine understanding between opposing governments or parties. People do not usually admit that they are issuing propaganda, and the word is much misused. Propaganda by one's own government or political party is described as a policy statement or as part of its news service; genuine approaches and statements of policy by another government or party are frequently dismissed as mere propaganda.

This is as true today as when it was written.

In order to succeed, public relations must be transparent, free from bias and demonstrate a two-way dynamic process where the aim is mutual understanding of the facts even if there is no subsequent agreement on policy or ideology. Organizations often need to respond to unfavourable criticism. Jefkins (1993) argued for an anatomy of public relations based on the transfer process, which shows an organization converting four negative states into positive ones, whereby hostility is converted into sympathy; prejudice into acceptance; apathy into interest; and ignorance into knowledge.

Ethical evaluation

Even within the UK National Health Service (NHS), which is held in such high esteem, there is still a lack of systematic ethical evaluation. The principles of the Declaration of Helsinki are relevant to the NHS or any organization in terms of efficacy, skill and reputation. The moral principles from the Declaration demonstrate that:

● any enquiry involving human participants should not occur unless aims and methods can achieve the stated and appropriate goals;
● any risk associated with human enquiry should always be proportional to its potential benefits, remembering that the interests and rights of individual participants should not be ignored in the name of the public good;
● individuals should not participate in human inquiry without their consent, after they have been given adequate information about the aims, methods, potential benefits, risks and other practical implications for them of their participation; and
● the confidentiality of individuals who participate in research should always be respected, irrespective of whether their participation is direct or indirect.

The moral importance of independent evaluation stems from the potential for researchers themselves to underestimate the problems associated with new campaign proposals. The best intentions can lead to improper aims and methods, along with unrecognized conflicts of interest. In the NHS, regional ethics committees are now well established and advise universities and individuals in every part of the UK.

However, an important aspect of sound ethical practice is transparency, which can be problematic in covert observation that may nevertheless be in the best interests of the public good, eg sociological research into activities of criminals. As Bryman states (2004: 520), the political dimensions of research are concerned with issues to do with the role and exercise of power, which links to a society or culture's value system, an increasingly complex issue in global ethical decision making for international organizations. Thus, today's leading corporate public relations directors and outsourced advisers and consultants are coaches, helping to create learning organizations. In the United States, they are referred to as 'counsellors'. They work with CEOs to balance risk during change and conflict by both goal setting (mission) and vision (statements) in line with sustainable development and continuity planning. Marketing publicity and promotion contribute to this in a creative but time-controlled manner in the selling of products and services.

In 2006 in the UK, the government was concerned that there would not be enough capital to develop Qinetiq, the research arm of the Ministry of Defence. So, that Spring, the company was floated on the London Stock Exchange, with only a 25 per cent share remaining with the Ministry of Defence and 75 per cent being held by private equity groups and other stakeholders. Journalist Andrew Gilligan wrote in the *London Evening Standard* (24 January 2006): 'if the company comes to be ruled by the bottom line, the risk is that Qinetiq will rest on its evaluation work and its already proven technologies, and some of that creativity will fade'. He cautioned Qinetiq is:

> a national treasure house of intellectual property and scientific endeavour that has until now been used to enrich the nation rather than its own senior management. Few other major governments, certainly not the Americans, have taken a similar route with their defence research bodies. Then there is the prospect of conflicts of interest.

There are key communication implications for different styles of corporate governance. In the West, most countries are divided into three groups, having monistic, dualistic and pluralistic concepts of their corporations based on their nation's history, economy, politics and culture. With emerging technological convergence, the level of skill involved in reassuring a country's public while retaining core cultural norms is a challenge to business leaders and their communication strategies. There is no reason why strategic thinking cannot be both logical and creative so long as it is ethical. Table 8.1 offers a rational thinking versus generative thinking perspective. Long-term public relations campaigns depend on generative thinking and diplomacy in the building of relations with governments, financial institutions such as the World Bank and non-governmental organizations (NGOs).

A current project managed by the UK government's Department for International Development is using the perspective of strategic communication to fight poverty through a long-term public relations process, which includes information dissemination, events, promotion of the concept itself, consultation, awareness raising, workshops, seminars and campaigns. Named the 'Poverty Reduction Strategy', the global project's public relations team argues that communication intervention is a prime element of their poverty reduction objective because participation of key stakeholders is one

Table 8.1 *Rational thinking vs generative thinking*

	Rational	*Generative*
Emphasis on	Logic over creativity	Creativity over logic
Cognitive style	Analytical	Intuitive
Reasoning follows	Formal, fixed rules	Informal, variable rules
Nature of reasoning	Computational	Imaginative
Direction of reasoning	Vertical	Lateral
Value placed on	Consistency and rigour	Unorthodoxy and vision
Reasoning hindered by	Incomplete information	Adherence to current ideas
Assumption about reality	Objective, (partially) knowable	Subjective, (partially) creatable
Decisions based on	Calculation	Judgement
Metaphor	Strategy as science	Strategy as art

Source: de Wit and Meyer (1999)

of the major characteristics in terms of partnership and country ownership during preparation and implementation. It recognizes that one of the critical elements of a strategic communication intervention is that communication activities are planned, designed, organized and implemented in a coherent, strategic manner. The strategic issues involve:

- identifying the sender of information for each communication activity;
- message development;
- confidence and trust;
- packaging the information;
- timing;
- sustaining momentum;
- quality and accuracy of information;
- follow-up and linkages;
- culture;
- language;
- attitudes and behaviour;
- institutional issues such as coordination and collaboration with other government and NGO departments and agencies;
- capacity-building;
- costing.

Some of the structural impediments to participation and country ownership are found in the underlying political culture, but access to information can also be a problem.

An important ethical definition is offered by the United Nations Development Programme, which states that:

> access to information is not only about promoting and protecting rights to information but is equally concerned with promoting and protecting communication (use of information) to voice one's views, to participate in democratic processes that take place at all levels (community, national, regional and global) and to set priorities for action. (UNDP, 2003: 3)

Communication within and between the key stakeholder groups is mapped as a framework for strategic communication, none of which is homogenous; see Figure 8.1.

An institutional theory perspective of strategic management underpins this corporate communication project using the process of isomorphism in the expectation that most stakeholders experience similar social expectations even where disparities of wealth are so marked.

The dynamic global environments in which organizations operate require multidimensional approaches to strategic management. From early military models to transaction cost economic models, global markets and e-commerce are reshaping strategic management theory and practice. Competition analysis now incorporates allowances, cooperative agreements and entrepreneurship, with the business model used and abused more widely than ever before. Public relations practitioners are central to an organization's strategy in matching company plans to the competitive environment with the organization's resources and capabilities.

Media stories on the troubles at Enron, Parmalot, MCI World Com and others have brought the issue of strategic management into sharp focus, giving some celebrity CEOs iconic status, while covering reams of newsprint about the role of expertise or lack of it, and personal and professional qualities essential to organizational success in the longer term. Economic and environmental pressures have once again raised the profile of corporate public relations and corporate communication's role in the boardroom as firms monitor and track micro and macro economies and environments in the face of threats to resources and prices. Annual reports, company statements and sound-bite clichés are scrutinized for efficiency and effectiveness from a social perspective. Opinion formers look to see if CEOs are committed to long-term sustainability of their organizations and have clear direction and tactics based on agreed behavioural and ethical standards. Their public relations advisers are supported in this role by the organization's own codes of conduct and ethics statements, as well as that of the professional Institute.

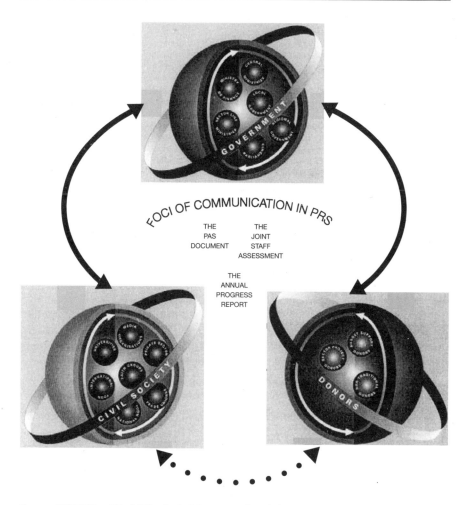

Source: DfID/The World Bank, in Mozammel and Odugbemi (2005)

Figure 8.1 *A framework for analysing strategic communication in the Poverty Reduction Strategy campaign*

The CIPR operates a code of professional conduct with disciplinary powers to which all members agree to adhere. The Professional Practices Committee of the Institute has occasion to handle complaints brought against members of the Institute who are thought to be in breach of the Code. In regard to the supply of public relations services, the Code emphasizes that honest and proper regard for the public interest, reliable and accurate information, and never misleading clients, employers and other professionals about the nature of representation or what can be competently delivered or achieved, are vital components of robust professional advice. A full Review of the Code is available online.

There can never be one theory or best practice approach to moral dilemmas because much will depend on individual and corporate value systems, but the role of aphorism in ethical theory allows for different morale values as well as allowing for basic social principles and rules to be incorporated into evaluation of decision making in business. Because morality is a social phenomenon, the ethical dimensions of corporate governance often lie squarely in the remit of the PR practitioner. Because of the different main board structures in Britain and continental Europe, the independence of non-executive board members can prove challenging to the public relations practitioner. Combined with IT overload, it can result in decision paralysis or inertia. The pragmatic public relations practitioner at board level will be expected to cope with conflicting viewpoints while retaining the ability to communicate symmetrically with all stakeholders in dealing with the ethics surrounding the business of globalization, citizenship and sustainability.

The PR strategist has to remain sensitive to the variety of situations that institutions and managers find themselves in that go beyond merely conforming to codified laws and procedures. In Europe, the last three decades of a market economy has driven PR practice to engage in new levels of ethical business practice that includes various concepts of corporate citizenship. This is leading to new conceptual frameworks for the core practice of public relations and conduct of corporate communication. It will be for the skilled, experienced and knowledgeable PR practitioner to ensure that the ethical codes being produced in great numbers are genuine and not later proven to be counterproductive to stakeholder relations, decision making and globalized democracy.

CAMPAIGN: DEUTSCHE POST WORLD NET, GERMANY

Deutsche Post World Net/DHL (DPWN) is the world's leading logistics company with 500,000 employees in more than 220 countries and territories.

'We deliver help' is the joint motto and the key promise of the long-term global cooperation between DPWN and UNICEF. The humanitarian programme was aimed to tackle one of the most vital issues of global society, the fight against child mortality, making use of the company's core competence in logistics and the potential of its global workforce. The programme offered a global platform to become socially engaged for all 500,000 employees, and thus enabled management and employees to live their social responsibility.

Communication in 2007 marked the first internal step of a multi-stage communication programme aimed at engaging employees at different levels to strengthen DPWN's global reputation and its 'licence to operate'. More than 50,000 employees informed themselves about engagement opportunities, tens of thousands took part in fundraising events, and over 600 aimed at becoming a volunteer in the Kenyan health project, laying the basis for the 2008 global rollout of the DPWN/ UNICEF partnership.

Challenge vs opportunity

The DPWN board of management was convinced that along with its global business operations comes global business responsibility and the need to develop strong and long-term strategic alliances. These should build on DPWN's key assets for employee motivation, talent and its core competences in logistics.

The company has a range of programmes that offer opportunities to volunteer in the Group's community programmes to:

- tackle questions of vital importance to global society;
- empower DPWN employees to help solving such problems being within their grasp;
- keep DPWN's global 'licence to operate' vital by sustaining employees' engagement and the company's reputation vis-á-vis its key stakeholders.

Corporate social responsibility (CSR) is a key element of DPWN's corporate culture, closely linked to the company's business strategy to meet its obligations of the financial markets.

DPWN entered into a global partnership with UNICEF in 2006, the same year it signed the Global Compact for the Group. The goal of the partnership was to provide UNICEF with long-term assistance in its worldwide fight to reduce child mortality. DPWN supported UNICEF by:

- providing the company's core competences in logistics as an in-kind donation;
- implementing a global donation and fundraising programme;
- enabling employee volunteers to support health-related UNICEF projects to benefit local communities.

Research

Several surveys, for example by the Industrial Society on UK staff recruitment, strongly emphasized that employees would rather work for companies that integrate CSR into their management systems and follow a consistent and holistic approach. Other studies, both in Europe and the US, supported these findings and emphasized the motivational aspects of employees' engagement and volunteering programmes.

The DPWN programme relied on fundamental data and field research of UNICEF and other UN organizations that gave proof of the outstanding ability of professional logistics and (especially last-mile) distribution to contribute to the global fight against poverty and deprivation (http://www.un.org/millenniumgoals/).

Strategic plan

The collaboration was launched in 2006 and first concentrated on projects in Kenya, the designated pilot country. Communication in 2007 marked the first, mainly internal, step of a multi-stage communication programme that was growing in parallel with the commitment of DPWN to support UNICEF's worldwide programme, 'Young Child Survival and Development' including Sub-Saharan Africa, the regions of Asia and South America. The international programme was expected to provide a sound basis for reputation management and was supported by an external communication programme in 2008.

The communication objectives changed focus in three phases during progression of the programme from spring to winter 2007 and became:

- launch by achieving global attention of all employees;
- implementation by engaging people inside and winning support outside DPWN;
- follow-up by sustaining effects and preparing groundwork for 2008.

Measurable criteria were related to the three thematic centres of the programme:

1. Donating and fundraising including the amount of employees' donations; number and intensity of fundraising events initiated by employees.
2. Volunteering such as the number of applicants for the limited volunteering opportunities.
3. Communicating the collaboration by increasing the number of downloads of the programme-related intranet articles, number of detailed feedbacks and requests; action taken by internal and/or external target groups to continue the UNICEF cooperation.

Target audiences were in the first instance the employees of DPWN worldwide, governmental bodies and NGOs relevant for the material success of the Kenyan pilot and actions required of them.

PR messages

- At DPWN 'corporate responsibility' is a personal commitment of management and employees.
- DPWN made use of its core competences to help local communities and society in responding to global challenges of vital importance and contributing to the Millennium Development Goals.
- DPWN is committed to goals that generate benefits for all the communities where the company operates.

Communication tactics

- Winning motivated and already engaged employees by offering a corporate platform to foster their social commitment.
- Inspiring interested employees to take action by offering a variety of alternatives and making use of committed employee 'ambassadors'.
- Communicating the programme's objectives, progress and impact on children and society to initiate further action.

Actions securing management's support of the campaign – regular reports on progress to the management board about the UN partnership.

Operational strategy

In 2007 the material and communicative objectives were realized through different instruments in a three-phase, three-centre communication programme; see Table 8.2.

Campaign outcomes

Material outcomes

Through employees' and company's support DPWN has helped UNICEF to achieve two of the UN's Millennium Development Goals (Goal 4 is to reduce child mortality by two thirds, Goal 6 is to combat HIV/AIDS, malaria and other diseases). In detail this meant for the 2007 'We deliver help' campaign, DPWN employees supported the UNICEF project in Kenya with the following.

In-kind and earmarked cash contribution, globally:

Table 8.2 *Operational strategy, DPWN*

1. Launch – achieving global attention

Donating and fundraising	*Volunteering*	*Communicating the collaboration*
Flyers, intranet-articles and direct communication calling for donations and organization of fundraising events	Internal multi-level selection process choosing 12 employees from 637 applications received from all regions and business divisions	International communication on DPWN UNICEF partnership during G8 Summit in June 2007

2. Implementation – engaging people and winning support

Donating and fundraising	*Volunteering*	*Communicating the collaboration*
Fundraising events (DHL Eurocup in Lommel/Belgium, Cleaning Cars for Good Cause in Kenya, Accounting of the yellow bull in Germany, Christmas karaoke in Germany)	16th and 28th September 2007 – twelve DPWN employees travelled to Kenya to support UNICEF in a health-related awareness campaign and to monitor the progression of the joint projects	International press release (September 18, 2007) – one year anniversary One year anniversary flyer – Thanks to donors and volunteers

3. Sustaining effects and following groundwork for 2008

Donating and fundraising	*Volunteering*	*Communicating the collaboration*
Fundraising Toolkit motivating and instructing employees to take more action in 2008 Instructions for employee ambassadors to support the donation and fundraising efforts	Volunteers' reports and diaries published via DPWN intranet	UNICEF report, December 2007 on progress of the partnership

- Support for UNICEF global 'Young Child Survival and Development' programme.
- Validation of the shake test in cooperation with the WHO.
- Storage services from UNICEF's warehouse hub in Panama to Latin America destinations.
- Complete review/analysis of logistics support for European-based warehousing and dispatching services for cards and gifts.

Pilot country Kenya:

- Project support for the DPWN initiative in Kwale district, including Social Mobilizing, Capacity Building and Service Delivery.
- Media support for social mobilization on child health issues, including support for launch events co-branding.
- Contribution for UNICEF to service the partnership (support cost).
- Purchase of three solar-powered fridges delivered to designated health centres.
- IT equipment for Kwale district health services – in-kind.
- Set-up and management of a community logistics centre and in-ventory management system in Kwale district.
- Emergency flights and transportation of medical goods throughout Kenya.

Volunteering:

- Road show 'Malezi Bora', child health and nutrition weeks.
- Help create mural paintings of health messages in a local hospital.
- Creating awareness and knowledge of health issues.
- Clean-up exercise with local community groups.
- Monitoring and promoting the use of bed nets.
- Conduct volleyball tournament to promote health educative activities.

Employee donation and fundraising campaign:

- Individual donations of more than €200,000 were achieved.
- The funds were used to support country-wide childcare and nutrition weeks in Kenya to promote awareness of basic health issues and to increase the attendance rate of health facilities.

Communicative outcomes

- 53,000 readers of intranet article on Kenya volunteering were the most read article ever;

- 20 DPWN fundraising events in different countries reached tens of thousands of employees;
- reports and diaries of all DPWN volunteers were published to a global audience of 130,000 DPWN intranet users;
- 20 articles in global, internal and external magazines, newsletters and online media road shows in Kenya reached more than 25,000 people directly;
- worldwide broadcast of two health education films took place;
- health and education projects worked as important communication and collaboration platforms with governmental bodies and NGOs in Kenya.

REFLECTION

Based on the information provided:

1. Does this case illustrate the complex boundaries between public relations vs propaganda; communication vs information; power vs influence?
2. Is Deutsche Post World Net likely to become increasingly dependent on rational or generative thinking of itself and of its stakeholders?
3. Does the Deutsche Post World Net approach to social responsibility offer sustainable values?
4. Is the Deutsche Post World Net monistic, dualistic or pluralistic in its approach to reputation management and ethical governance?
5. Do Deutsche Post World Net's evaluation outcomes suggest the programme is working well enough for the operational strategy to help sustain UNICEF's development goals 4 and 6 over time?

CIPR CODE OF CONDUCT

The CIPR operates an enduring yet evolving Code of Professional Conduct to which all members adhere. The Professional Practices Committee of the Institute handles complaints against members of the Institute who may be in breach of the Code, and has disciplinary powers.

This extract emphasizes vital components of robust professional practice, such as honest and proper regard for the public interest; reliable and accurate information; and never misleading clients, employers or other professionals about the nature of representation or what can be competently delivered or achieved.

PRINCIPLES FOR MAINTAINING PROFESSIONAL STANDARDS

- Maintain the highest standards of professional endeavour, integrity, confidentiality, financial propriety and personal conduct.
- Deal honestly and fairly in business with employers, employees, clients, fellow professionals, other professions and the public.
- Respect the customs, practices and codes of clients, employers, colleagues, fellow professionals and other professions in all countries where they practise.
- Take all reasonable care to ensure employment best practice including giving no cause for complaint of unfair discrimination on any grounds.

- Work within the legal and regulatory frameworks affecting the practice of public relations in all countries where they practise.
- Encourage professional training and development among members of the profession.
- Respect and abide by this Code and related Notes of Guidance issued by the Institute of Public Relations and encourage others to do the same.

ONLINE SOURCES

In alphabetical order, these are:

www.65.214.34.30/un/gc/unweb.nsf/content/thenine.htm
www.area.sutantoputra@buseco.monesh.edu.au
www.bsbs.co.uk
www.caseplace.org
www.chime.plc.uk/downloads/reputationkm.pdf
www.cipr.co.uk
www.cmocouncil.org
www.corporatecomm.org/conference.html
www.criticaleye.net
www.diomo.com
www.ecch.com
www.emeraldinsight.com/ccij.htm
www.gmj.gallup.com/content/default.asp?ci=466
www.ipra.org
www.nao.gov.uk
www.nla.co.uk
www.pmi.org
www.reputationinstitute.com
www.runepeitersen.com/saccadic or www.runepeitersen.com
www.sru.soc.surrey.ac.uk.sru49.html
www.standard.co.uk/anthonyhilton
www.standard.co.uk/chrisblackhurst

www.timesonline.co.uk/tol/comment/columnists/andrew_sullivan
www.tvu.ac.uk
www.watsonwyatt.com/research/resrender.asp?id=w-698&page=1
www.worldinblance.net/agreements/1961-vienna-diplomaticrelations.php

BIBLIOGRAPHY

Allison, G T (1971) *Essence of Decision Making*, Little Brown, New York

Allison, R E (1993) *Global Disasters: Inquiries into Management Ethics*, Prentice Hall, Harlow

Alsop, R J (2004) *The 18 Immutable Laws of Corporate Reputation*, Kogan Page, London

Atkinson (1985) The changing corporation, in (ed) D Clutterbuck, *New Patterns of Work*, Gower, Aldershot

Aufderheide, P (1999) *Communications Policy & The Public Interest*, Guilford, London

Aula, P and Mantere, S (2008) *Strategic Reputation Management*, Routledge, London

Aurila, L (1993) Stakeholder Ethics, University of Helsinki Conference Paper, in (ed) S Oliver (1997) *Corporate Communication*, Kogan Page, London

Baerns, B and Raupp, J (2002) Modelling and evaluating public relations campaigns, in (eds) H-D Klingemann and A Römmele, *Public Information Campaigns and Opinion Research: A handbook for the student and practitioner*, Sage, London

Barrass, R (2002) *Scientists Must Write*, Routledge, London

Barrett, D J (2004) A best practice approach to designing a change management programme, Ch. 2, Part I, in (ed) S Oliver, *Handbook of Corporate Communication and Public Relations: Pure and applied*, Routledge, London

Baskin, O, Aronoff, C and Lattimore, D (1997) *Public Relations*, 4th edn, Brown & Benchmark, Madison, WI

Bennett, R (1996) *Corporate Strategy & Business Planning*, Pitman, London

Bent, N – see Online Sources, www.demos.co.uk.

Berger, B K and Reber, B H (2006) *Gaining Influence in Public Relations: The role of resistance in practice*, Lawrence Erlbaum, New Haven

Bernays, E L (1923) *Crystallizing Public Opinion*, Liveright, US

Bernstein, D (1991) *Company Image and Reality*, Cassell, London

Berridge, G R (2004) *Diplomacy: Theory and Practice*, 2nd edn, Macmillan, London

Boje, D M (2001) *Narrative Methods for Organisational and Communication Research*, Sage, London

Boorstin, D (1963) *The Image or What Happened to the American Dream*, Penguin, Harmondsworth

Botan, C H and Hazleton, V (eds) (2006) *Public Relations Theory II*, Lawrence Erlbaum, New Haven

Boulding, E (1956) *The Image*, The University of Michigan Press, Ann Arbor, MI

Bovee, C L, Thill, J V and Schatzman, B E (2003) *Business Communication Today*, 7th edn, Prentice Hall, Harlow

Braam, G J M and Nijssen, E J (2004) Performance effects of using the balanced scorecard: a note on the Dutch experience, *Long Range Planning*, **37,** 4, August, Elsevier, Oxford

Brooking, A (1996) *Intellectual Capital/Core asset for the third millennium enterprise*, Thompson Business, London

Broom, G M and Dozier, D M (eds) (1990) *Using Research in Public Relations*, Prentice Hall, Harlow

Brouthers, K D (1995) Strategic alliances: choose your partners, *Long Range Planning*, **28,** 3, pp 18–25

Bryman, A (2004) *Social Research Methods*, 2nd edn, Oxford University Press, Oxford

Chesborough, H W and Teece, D J (1996) When is virtual virtuous: organizing for innovation, *Harvard Business Review*, January–February

Christians, C and Traeber, M (1997) *Communication Ethics and Universal Values*, Sage, London

Christopher, M, Payne, A and Ballantyne, D (1994) *Relationship Marketing*, Butterworth-Heinemann, Oxford

CIFAS (2009) *Staff Fraud Database Figures*, CIFAS, London

CIPR/MORI/Business in the Community (2002) *Reputation and the Bottom Line*, CIPR, London

Clampitt, P G (2001) *Communicating for Managerial Effectiveness*, 2nd edn, Sage, London

Clowe, K E and Baack, D (2004) *Integrated Advertising, Promotion & Marketing Communications*, 2nd edn, Pearson Prentice Hall, Harlow

Cornelissen, J (2004) *Corporate Communications Theory and Practice*, Sage, London

Crane, A and Matten, D (2004) *Business Ethics: A European perspective*, Oxford University Press, Oxford

Craven, D W (1994) *Strategic Marketing*, 4th edn, Irwin, New York

Crossman, A and McIlwee, T (1995) *Signalling Discontent: A study of the 1994 signal workers' dispute*, Thames Valley University School of Management, London

Crow, D (2003) *Visible Signs: An introduction to semiotics*, AVA, Worthing

Davidson, H (2005) *The Committed Enterprise*, 2nd edn, Elsevier, Oxford

Davis, A (2002) *Public Relations Democracy*, Manchester University Press, Manchester

Davis, A (2004) *Mastering Public Relations*, Palgrave Macmillan, Basingstoke

de Wit, B and Meyer, R (1999) *Strategy Synthesis: Resolving strategy paradoxes to create competitive advantage*, Thompson Learning, London

Dowling, C (1993) Developing your company image into a corporate asset, *Long Range Planning*, **26**, pp 101–9

Durant, A (2008) *Times Higher Education Supplement*, 10 July, p 51

Eco, U (1989) *The Open Work*, Harvard University Press, Harvard MA

Ehling, W P (1985) Application of decision theory in the construction of a theory of public relations management, II, *Public Relations Research and Education*, **2**, 1, pp 4–22, in (eds) G M Broom and D M Dozier, *Using Research in Public Relations*, Prentice Hall, Harlow

Eiser, J R (1980) *Cognitive Social Psychology*, McGraw-Hill, Maidenhead

Elliott, F (1975) *A Dictionary of Politics*, Penguin, Harlow

Engler, P (1992) Building transnational alliances to create competitive advantage, *Long Range Planning*, **25**, 1

Ewing, M T, Caruana, A and Loy, E R (1999) Corporate reputation and perceived risk in professional engineering services, *Corporate Communication International Journal*, **4**, 3, pp 121–8

Fayol, H (1987) *General & Industrial Management*, Irwin, New York

Fearn-Banks, K (2001) *Crisis Communications: A casebook approach*, LEA, New York

Fernandez, J (2004) *Corporate Communications*, Sage, London

Fill, C (2006) *Marketing Communication*, 4th edn, FT Prentice Hall, Harlow

Fill, C (2009) *Marketing Communications: Interactivity, communities and content*, 5th edn, Pearson Education, Oxford

Florence, B T and Kovacic, B (2001) Intersections between Crisis and Management: A case study, pp 81–90 in (eds) D P Cushmand and S Sanderson King, *Excellence in Communications Organizational Strategy*, SUNY Press, New York

Fryxell, G E and Wang, J (1994) The Fortune's Corporate Reputation Index: reputation of what?, *Journal of Management*, **20**, 1, pp 1–14

Galetzka, M, Gelders, D, Verckens, J P and Seydel, E (2008) Transparency and performance communication: a case study of Dutch Railways, *Corporate Communication: An International Journal*, **13**, p 4

Gao, Y (2008) An ethical judgement framework for corporate political actions, *Journal of Public Affairs*, **8**, 4, 153–63

Gaunt, R and Wright, D (2008) *PR Measurement*, Benchpoint, London

Gaved, M (1997) Corporate governance, the challenge for communication practitioners, *Corporate Communication International Journal*, **2** (2)

George, M W (2008) *The Elements of Library Research: What every student needs to know*, Princeton University Press

Gorb, P (1992) The psychology of corporate identity, *European Management Journal*, **10**, p 310

Goudge, P (2006) *Employee Research*, Kogan Page, London

Grant, A W H and Schlesinger, L A (1995) Realize your customer's full profit potential, *Harvard Business Review*, September–October, pp 59–72

Greenwood, J (2005) *Essential Law for Journalists*, 18th edn, Oxford University Press, Oxford

Gregerson, H B, Morrison, A J and Black, J S (1999) Leaders for the global frontier, *Frontline*, **21**, 4

Grunig, J E (1992) *Excellence in Public Relations and Communication Management*, Lawrence Erlbaum, New Haven

Grunig, J E (2006) Furnishing the edifice: ongoing research on public relations as a strategic management function, *Journal of Public Relations Research*, **18**, 2

Grunig, J E and Hunt, T (1984) *Managing Public Relations*, Holt, Rinehart & Winston, New York

Grunig, J E and Repper, F C (1992) Strategic management, publics and issues, in J E Grunig, *Excellence in Public Relations and Communication Management*, Lawrence Erlbaum, New Haven

Grunig, J E and White, J (1992) The effect of world views on public relations theory & practice in (ed) J E Grunig, *Excellence in Public Relations and Communication Management*, Lawrence Erlbaum, New Jersey

Grunig, L A, Grunig, J E and Dozier, D M (2002) *Organizations: A study in three countries*, Lawrence Erlbaum, New Haven

Gugler, P (1992) Building transnational alliances to create competitive advantage, *Long Range Planning*, **25**, 1, pp 90–99

Guiltinan, J P and Paul, G W (1994) *Marketing Management: Strategies and programmes*, 5th edn, McGraw-Hill, Maidenhead

Hannigan, T (2005) *Management Concepts and Practices*, 4th edn, FT Prentice Hall, Harlow

Hannington, T (2004) *How to Measure and Manage Your Corporate Reputation*, Gower, Aldershot

Hargie, O (ed) (2006) *The Handbook of Communication Skills*, 3rd edn, Routledge, Oxford

Hayes, A F (2005) *Statistical Methods for Communication Science*, Lawrence Erlbaum, New Haven

Hearit, K (2006) *Crisis Management by Apology: Corporate response to allegations of wrongdoing*, Lawrence Erlbaum, New Haven

Hendy, D (2008) *Life on Air: A history of Radio Four*, Oxford University Press, Oxford

Herstein, R, Mitki, Y and Jaffe, E D (2008) Communicating a new corporate image during privatization: the case of El Al airlines, *Corporate Communications International Journal*, **13**, 4

Hofstede, G H (1991) *Cultures and Organizations*, McGraw-Hill, Maidenhead

Holman, D and Thorpe, R (2003) *Management & Language*, Sage, London

Houlden, B (1988) The corporate conscience, *Management Today*, August

Hrasky, S and Smith, B (2008) Concise corporate reporting: communication or symbolism?, *Corporate Communication: An International Journal*, **13**, p 4

Illegems, V and Verbeke, A (2004) Telework: what does it mean for management?, *Long Range Planning*, **37**, 4

Ind, N (1997) *The Corporate Brand*, Macmillan Business Press, London

Institute for Public Policy Research – see Online Sources: www.ippr.org. uk/publicationsandreports/publication.asp?id=646

Investor Relations Society – see Online Sources: www.ir-soc.org.uk/index. asp?pageid=249

Jefkins, F (1993) *Planned Press and Public Relations*, Blackie, Edinburgh

Jenkins, M and Ambrosini with Collier, N (2007) *Advanced Strategic Management: A multi-perspective approach*, 2nd edn, Palgrave Macmillan, Basingstoke

Jessup, L and Valacich (2006) *Information Systems Today: Why IS matters*, 2nd edn, Pearson Prentice Hall, Harlow

Jobber, D (1995) *Principles and Practice of Marketing*, McGraw-Hill, Maidenhead

Johnson, G and Scholes, K (2002) *Exploring Corporate Strategy*, 6th edn, Prentice Hall, Harlow

Jolly, V (1996) Global strategies in the 1990s, Mastering Management Series no 5, *Financial Times*, London

Jørgensen, P E F and Isaksson, M (2008) Building credibility, *International Banking and Financial Markets, Corporate Communications: An International Journal*, **13**, p 4

Kaid, L L (ed) (2004) *Handbook of Political Communication Research*, Lawrence Erlbaum, New Haven

Kaplan, R S and Norton, D P (2001) *The Strategy-focused Organization*, Harvard Business School Press, Boston, MA

Kay, J (1999) Strategy and the delusion of grand designs, in (eds) A Huczynski and D Buchanan, *Organisation Behaviour*, FT/Prentice Hall, Harlow

Kimmel, A J (2004) *Rumours and Rumour Control*, Lawrence Erlbaum, New Haven

Kirban, L and Jackson, B C (1990) Using research to plan programmes, in (eds) G M Broom and D M Dozier, *Using Research in Public Relations*, Prentice Hall, Harlow

Koter, P and Mirdak, W (1978) Marketing and public relations, *Journal of Marketing*, **42**, 4, pp13–20

Kotler, P (1988) *Marketing Management: Analysis, planning, implementation and control*, Prentice Hall, Harlow

Kotler, P (1994) *Marketing Management,* 8th edn, Prentice Hall, Harlow

Kotler, P, Armstrong, G, Saunders, J and Wong, V (1999) *Principles of Marketing*, 2nd European edn, Prentice Hall, Harlow

Krajewski, LJ and Ritzman, LP (2002) *Operations Management: Strategy & analysis*, 6th edn, Prentice Hall, Harlow

Lerbinger, O (2006) *Corporate Public Affairs: Interacting with interest groups, media and governments*, Lawrence Erlbaum, New Haven

Lerbinger, O and Sullivan, A J (1965) *Information, Influence and Communication*, Basic Books, New York

L'Etang, J and Pieczka, M (2006) *Public Relations: Critical debates and contemporary practice*, Lawrence Erlbaum, New Haven

Liew, J (1997) Banking on a sharper image?, *Corporate Communication International Journal,* **2**, 2, 76–86

Luftman, J N (2004) *Managing the Information Technology Resource: Leadership in the information age*, Pearson Prentice Hall, Harlow

Luftman, J N *et al* (2004) *Managing the Information Technology Resource: Leadership in the Information Age*, Pearson Prentice Hall, Harlow

Lynch, K (1991) *The Image of the City*, MIT Press, Cambridge, MA

Maathuis, O J M (1993) *Corporate Image, Performance and Communication*, Eburon, Delft

McKenzie, J and van Winkelen, C (2004) *Understanding the Knowledge Organization*, Thomson, London

Mackiewicz, A (1993) *Guide to Building a Global Image*, McGraw-Hill, Maidenhead

McMaster, M (1996) Foresight: exploring the structure of the future, *Long-Range Planning,* **29**, 2, pp 149–55

McQuail, D (1994) *Mass Communication Theory*, Sage, London

Macrae, C (1991) *World Class Brands*, Addison-Wesley, London

Malmelin, N (2007) Communication capital: modelling corporate communications as an organisational asset, *Corporate Communication, An International Journal,* **10**, p 310

Mast, C (2005) Creating values by communication, in (eds) J Pfannenberg and A Zerfass, *Creating Economic Value through Communication*, pp 27–35, Frankfurter Allgemeine Buch, Frankfurt

Mayer, M (1961) *Madison Avenue*, Penguin, Harmondsworth

Meijer, M-M (2004) *Does Success Breed Success? Effects of news and advertising on corporate reputation*, Aksant, Amsterdam

Messina, A (2007) Public relations, the public interest and persuasion: an ethical approach, *Corporate Communication, An International Journal,* **10**, p 310

Mintzberg, H and Quinn, J B (eds) (1996) *The Strategy Process: Concepts, contexts, cases*, 3rd edn, Prentice Hall, Harlow

Mintzberg, H, Ahlstrand, B and Lampel, J (1998) *Strategy Safari: A guided tour through the wilds of strategic management*, The Free Press, New York

Morgan, G (1997) *Images of Organization*, Sage, London

Mozammel, M and Odugbemi, S (eds) (2005) *With the Support of Multitudes*, Information and Communication for Development, DFID/Development Communication Division, External Affairs, The World Bank, New York

Mutch, A (2008) *Managing Knowledge and Information in Organizations: A literacy approach*, Routledge, London

Newman, W (1956) Basic objectives which shape the character of a company, *The Journal of Business*, **26,** 211

Nornes, R (2007) Aon Risk Report – see Online Sources

Olaniran, B A and Williams, D E (2001) Anticipatory model of crisis management, in (ed) R L Heath, *Handbook of Public Relations*, Sage, London

Oliver, S (1996) Perceptions and practice of corporate communication in small businesses, *Corporate Communication: An International Journal*, **1,** 2

Oliver, S (1997) *Corporate Communication: Principles, Techniques and Strategies*, Kogan Page, London

Oliver, S (1998) Technology assisted teaching and learning: design implications for communication courses on the internet, *Journal of Communication Management*, **3,** 1

Oliver, S (2000a) Message from the CEO: a three minute rule?, *Corporate Communication: An International Journal*, **5,** 3

Oliver, S (2000a) Symmetrical communication: does reality support rhetoric?, *Corporate Communication: An International Journal*, **5,** 1

Oliver, S (2001) *Public Relations Strategy*, Kogan Page, London

Oliver, S (2002) A crisis of confidence: M&S plc, in (eds) D Moss and B De Santo, *Public Relations Cases: International Perspectives*, Routledge, London

Oliver, S (2004a) Communicating a continuity plan: the action stations framework, in (ed) S Oliver, *Handbook of Corporate Communication and Public Relations: Pure and applied*, Routledge, London

Oliver, S (ed) (2004b) *Handbook of Corporate Communication and Public Relations: Pure and applied*, Routledge, London

Oliver, S (2006) *Public Relations Strategy*, 2nd edn, Kogan Page, London

Oliver, S (2008) *Public Relations Strategy*, 2nd revised edn, Kogan Page, London

Orna, E (2004) *Information in Strategy and Practice*, Aldershot, Gower

O'Sullivan, T, Hartley, J, Saunders, D, Montgomery, M and Fiske, J (1994) *Key Concepts in Communication and Cultural Studies*, Routledge, London

Parekh, B (2008) *A New Politics of Identity*, Palgrave Macmillan, Basingstoke

Pearce, J A II and Robinson, R B Jr (1982) *Strategic Management: strategy formulation and implementation*, Irwin, New York

Petrash, G (1996) Dow's journey to a knowledge value management culture, *European Management Journal*, **14,** 4, pp 365–73

Pettinger, R (2004) *Contemporary Strategic Management*, Palgrave Macmillan, Basingstoke

Pickton, D and Broderick, A (2005) *Integrated Marketing Communications*, 2nd edn, Pearson Education Ltd, Harlow

Porter, M (1985) *Competitive Advantage*, Free Press, New York

Poynter Institute's EyeTrack07 Study – see Online Sources, www.eyetrack.poynter.org

Price, A (2004) *Human Resource Management in a Business Context*, 2nd edn, Thomson, London

PricewaterhouseCoopers (2006) Global Private Equity Report – see Online Sources www.pwc.com

Quinn, J B *et al* (1996) Managing professional intellect: making the most of the best, *Harvard Business Review*, March-April, pp 71–80

Quinn, R E, Faerman, S R, Thompson, M P and McGrath, M R (2003) *Becoming a Master Manager: A competency framework*, 3rd edn, Wiley, Chichester

Rana, K S (2004) *The 21st Century Ambassador*, Oxford University Press, New Delhi

Regester, M and Larkin, J (2007) *Risk Issues and Crisis Management in Public Relations*, Kogan Page, London

Reich, R B (1990) Who is us?, *Harvard Business Review*, January–February

Reputation Institute (RI), Global Reputation Pulse™, Report (2008) – see Online Sources: www.reputationinstitute.com/knowledge-centre/global-pulse

Robbins, S P and Decenzo, D A (2004) *Fundamentals of Management*, 4th edn, Pearson Prentice Hall, Harlow

Roberts, C, Weetman, P and Gordon, P B (2008) *International corporate reporting, A comparative approach*, 4th revised edn, Prentice Hall, Harlow

Rogers, C (1993) Theory of personality and behaviour, in (eds) A Huczynski and D Buchanan, *Organisation Behaviour*, FT/Prentice Hall, Harlow

Rowson, R (2006) *Working Ethics: How to be fair in a culturally complex world*, Jessica Kingsley, London

Sanghi, S (2004) *The Handbook of Competency Mapping*, Sage, London

Schuster, C P and Copeland, M J (2008) Cultural theory in use: the intersection of structure process and communication in business practice, *Journal of Public Affairs*, **8**, 4, pp 261–80

Shuy, R W (2008) *Fighting Over Words: Language and civil law cases*, Oxford University Press, Oxford

Singer, P (1993) *Practical Ethics*, Cambridge University Press, Cambridge

Sjöstrand, S-E, Sandberg, J and Tyrstrup, M (2001) *Invisible Management: The social construction of leadership*, Thomson Learning, London

Smith, A and O'Neill, G (1997) Seamless marketing communications, in *CBI Corporate Communication Handbook*, Kogan Page, London

Soloman, M R, Marshall, G W and Stuart, E W (2006) *Marketing: Real people, real choices*, 4th edn, Pearson Prentice Hall, Harlow

Solove, D J (2008) The future of reputation, in (ed) P Gass, *Rumour and Privacy on the Internet*, Yale University Press, Cambridge MA

Sopow, E (1994) *The Critical Issues Audit*, Issue Action Publications, USA

Stacey, R D (1991) *The Chaos Frontier: Creative strategic control for business*, Butterworth-Heinemann, Oxford

Stacey, R D (1993) *Strategic Management and Organisational Dynamics*, Pitman, London

Stacks, D W (2002) *Primer of Public Relations Research*, The Guilford Press

Stanley, J (1991) Market communications, *European Management Journal*, **9**, 329–33

Steele, G R (2009) Letters to the editor/opinion, *The Times*, 7 February, p 21

Stuart, H (1999) Towards a definitive model of the corporate identity management, *Corporate Communication: An International Journal*, **4**, 4, pp 200–207

Sullivan, A (2009) *The Sunday Times*

Susskind, L and Field, P (1996) *Dealing with an Angry Public*, Free Press, New York

Sutantoputra, A W (2009) Social disclosure rating system for assessing firm's CSR reports, *Corporate Communications: An International Journal*, **14**, 1, p 34

Swart, J, Mann, C, Brown, S and Price, A (2005) *Human Resource Development*, Elsevier Butterworth Heinemann, Oxford

Thomas, C S and Hrebenar, R J (2008) Understanding interest groups, lobbying and lobbyists in developing democracies, *Journal of Public Affairs*, **8**, 1–2, pp 1–14

Thompson, J L (1995) *Strategy in Action*, Chapman & Hall, London

Toffler, A (1970) *Future Shock: A study of mass bewilderment in the face of accelerating change*, Bodley Head, London

Toth, E L (ed) (2006) *The Future of Excellence in Public Relations and Communication Management: Challenges for the next generation*, Lawrence Erlbaum, New Haven

The Turnbull Report (1999) *Internal Control: Guidance for Directors on the Combined Code*, The FRC, London

United Nations Development Programme (UNDP) (2003) – see Online Sources www.un.org/en/development

van den Bosch, A L M, de Jong, M D and Elving, W J L (2005) How corporate visual identity supports reputation, *Corporate Communication: An International Journal*, **10**, 2, p 108

van Riel, C B M (1995) *Principles of Corporate Communication*, Prentice Hall, Harlow

van Riel, C B M and Fombrun, C J (2007) *Essentials of Corporate Communication*, Routledge, London

van Ruler, B, Vercic, A T and Vercic, D (eds) (2008) *Public Relations Metrics: Research and evaluation*, Routledge, London

Walker, J, Holloway, I and Wheeler, S (2005) *Research Ethics Review*, **1**, 3, p 92

Wang, Y D and Emurian, H H (2005) An overview of online trust, *Computers in Human Behaviour*, **21**, pp 105–25

Weintraub, A E and Pinkleton, B E (2006) *Planning and Managing Effective Communication Programs*, 2nd edn, Lawrence Erlbaum, New Haven

White, C (2004) *Strategic Management*, Palgrave Macmillan, Basingstoke

White, J and Dozier, D M (1992) Public relations and management decision making, in (ed) J E Grunig, *Excellence in Public Relations and Communication Management*, Lawrence Erlbaum, New Haven

Whittington, R (2001) *What is Strategy – and does it matter?*, Thomson Learning, London

Williams, H M (1997) Financial relations, in (eds) O W Baskin, C Aronoff and D Lattimore, *Public Relations, The profession and the practice*, McGraw-Hill, Harlow

Wines, W A (2006) *Ethics, Law and Business*, Lawrence Erlbaum, New Haven

Zerfass, A (2008) Corporate communication revisited: integrating business strategy and strategic communication, in (eds) A Zerfass, B van Ruler and K Sriramesh, *Public Relations Research, European perspectives and international innovations*, Euprera, Wiesbaden

Zhu, J H and Blood, D (1997) Media agenda setting, in (ed) F M Kovacic, *Emerging Theories of Human Communication*, SUNY Press, New York

INDEX

NB: page numbers in *italic* indicate figures or tables

Accenture business risk management
    process 60
Acorn Consumer classification 147
Action research *13*
Action Stations Framework 47, *48–49*
Advertising, Institute of 101
Allison, G T 53, 58–59
American Pointer Institute 140
analyses
    cost-benefit 137
    intertextuality 144–45, *145, 146*
    PESTLE 42
    qualitative data 137
Annual Golden World Award (IPRA)
    xiii
Atkinson 91
    and flexible firm model 91

balanced scorecard 135–36, *136*
    Corporate Communications
        Scorecard (CCS) 136
Barrass, R 145
Barrett, D J *91*
Baskin, O 15

belief systems and attitude 72
Bennett, R 2
Bent, N 60
Bernays, E 16
Bernstein, D 72, 73
blogs/blogging 140, 141, 143
Blood, D 55
Boje, D M 138, 144
Bonfire of the Vanities 29
Boorstin, D 72, 74
Boulding, E 73
Braam, G J M 135, *136*
brand
    image 72
    promotion 111
branding theory 111
Broderick, A *104*
Brooking, A 45
Brouthers, K D 46
    and Four Cs of international strategic
        alliances 46, *46*
Bryman, A 134, 155
Business Communicators, International
    Association of (IABC) 16

business continuity planning, websites
for   62
business re-engineering   32

Cadbury Report   59
campaign: Accenture, Germany
148–51
challenge vs opportunity   148
operational strategy for   149–50
outcomes   150–51
research for   148–49
strategic plan for   149
campaign: American Airlines (US)
94–98
audience analysis for   96
challenge vs opportunity   95
operational strategy for   96–97
outcomes   97–98
research for   95
strategic plan for   96
campaign: Deutsche Postworld Net,
Germany   160–64
challenge vs opportunity   161
operational strategy for   163, *164*
outcomes   163, 165–66
research for   161–62
strategic plan for   162–63
campaign: Electrotechnical University
'Leti'   80–85, *83*
challenge vs opportunity   81
consultative action taken for   83
operational strategy for   84
outcomes   84–85
research for   81
strategic plan for   82–83, *83*
campaign: Global Peace Index
126–28
campaign: Hitachi GST (Japan)
114–17
challenge vs opportunity   115
operational strategy for   116–17
outcomes   117
research for   115
strategic plan for   116
campaign: Nestlé 'Make Space' 22–25
challenge vs opportunity   22
operational strategy for   24
outcomes   25

research for   22
strategic plan for   23–24
campaign: Partnership of Disaster
Response (US)
challenge vs opportunity   66
outcomes   69
research for   66–67
strategic plan for   67–69
CEO as cultural icon   37–38
Chambers, P   29
change
communicating   89–90
development plans   90
Chartered Accountants in England and
Wales, Institute of (ICAEW)   59
Chesborough, H W   47
Christians, C   153
Christopher, M   111, *113*
CIPR   5, 10, 16, 55, 74, 101, 123, 148
Code of Conduct   xiii, 167–68
and copyright   132
definition of PR   11, 154
Delphi Survey   1
OFR framework   43–44, *44*
policy   131
Professional Practices Committee of
159
cognition and behaviour, theories of   4
cognitive dissonance   34–35
communication   38 *see also* internal
communication *and* mass
communication
change strategy   *91*
corporate   11, 64–65
global   77
management models   57
performance indicators   and
strategic management   92–93
strategy   77, 90
as team effort   93–94
theories of mass   4
theory   103
competitive advantage   104–07
computer viruses and Y2K crisis
63–64 *see also* risk management
conceptual authenticity   100–01
conflict, coping with   34–35
consequentialism   77–78

continuity planning   62–65
continuous professional development
   (CPD)   xiii, 10
copyright   122
core governance (and)   27–70 *see also*
   management
   campaign: Partnership of Disaster
      Response (US) *see main entry*
   CEO as cultural icon   37–38
   cognitive dissonance *see main entry*
   communicating risk   40–43, 43
   continuity planning   62–70, 63, 65
   corporate governance   58–62, 62
   costing communication   28–31, 28,
      29, 30
   crisis and resilience
      management   47–50, 48–49
   function to strategy   31–34, 31, 32, 33
   managerial perception   56–58, 57, 58
   performance assessment   39–40, 39
   reputation vs operating and financial
      review   43–45, 44
   strategic alliances   45–47, 46
   writers' views on   50–56, 52, 53
corporate
   advertising   111
   identity   77
   mission   38
   personality theory   74–75
Corporate Reputation Institute (CRI)
   74–75
corporate social responsibility
   (CSR)   161
   social disclosure rating systems for
      PR programming   80
corporate visual identity   75
cost-benefit analysis measurement   137
Cravens, D W   111
'Creating Quality Dialogue' (DTI, UK)
   61
crises   21
crisis management   51–55
   London Stock Exchange   61
   for major emergencies   54–55
   major emergency plan for (MEP)   54
crisis prevention   51–54
   and rigidity and control   51–52
Crossman, A   90

Crow, D   76
cultural web   33
customer relations   107–08

data, collating methods for PR   30
data collection   106
   and methodological principles
      12–13
data-mining and loss of privacy   56
Days, M   141
de Sanssure, F   76
de Wit, B   157
decision making   92
Declaration of Helsinki and moral
   principles   155
defining
   environmental factors affecting
      corporate business   14
   IC as formula   45
definition(s) (of)   11, 154
   alternative practitioner   11
   celebrity   71
   corporate image   73
   ethical (UN Development
      Programme)   158
   extraordinary management   35
   identity   71
   image   71
   public relations   1, 11
   public relations (CIPR)   43, 154
   public relations (Mexican
      statement)   154
   reputation   71
   strategy   2–4
   traits of corporate personality   74–75
Dennehy   138
Derrider, J   138
Dow Chemical Company   45
Dowling, C   77
Dozier, D M   37, 39
Durant, A   144

Echo Research   79
Eco, U   76
Ehling, W P   153
Eiser, J R   72
employee communication strategy   90
environmental scanning   102

ethics 77, 153–66
  campaign: Deutsche Post World Net,
    Germany *see main entry*
  and Declaration of Helsinki 155
  evaluation 155–60, *157, 159*
  and PR vs propaganda 154–55
European Convention 56
European Directive on fair review
  42–43, *43*
Ewing, M T 79–80
exchange theory 92
eye-tracking 109, *109, 110*, 126,
  140–41, *142, 143*
  and EyeTrack07 141
  and MobileEye 141

Fayol, H 55
Fearn-Banks, K 51
feedback 16, 20–21
Field, P 56
Financial Services Authority (UK) 61
Financial Standard Authority (FSA)
  61
Financial Times 109, *109, 110*
Financial Times/PricewaterhouseCooper
  and seven-factor business
    performance model 78
flexible firm model 91
Florence 55, 56, 57
Fortune 78
  Fortune 500 companies 99
  Corporate Reputation Index 78
forecast plans – purveyance (Fayol)
  55
fraud prevention service (CIFAS, UK)
  64
Frysell, G E 78
FTSE-100 companies 27
Future Shock 101

Gaunt, R 137
Gaved, M 50–51
geo-demographic systems/research
  lists 147
Germany 'Land of Ideas'
  campaign 76–77
Gilligan, A 156
Global Reporting Initiative (GRI) 80

globalization 5, 124–25
  and communication 77
goodwill 43, 45
Goodwin, Sir F 29
Gorb, P 73
Grant, A W H 36
Greenpeace 123
Gregerson *29*
grounded theory 137–38
Grunig, J E 7, 15–16, 34, 35, 38, 107
Guiltinan, J P 103

Hampel Report 59
Hilton, A 29
Houlden, B 77
human resource management (HRM)
  88–89, 92, 93–94
Human Rights Act (1998) 91
Hunt, T 15
Hurley, R 64

identity fraud 64
Illegems, V 134–35
Ind, N 16, 17, 20, 121
Information Week 21
integrated marketing communication
  (IMC) mix model 103, *104*
intellectual capital management 45
internal communication (and) 87–98
  campaign: American Airlines (US) *see*
    main entry
  change development plans 90
  communicating change 89–90
  as core competency 88–89
  fairness vs flexibility 91–93
  morale 87–88
  privacy/confidentiality 88
  as team effort 93–94
internet 16, 39, 77, 124
Investor Relations Journal 60
Investor Relations Society 61
issues management *see* crisis
  management

Jackson, B C 153
Japan: Ministry of International Trade
  and Industry (MITI) 46
Jefkins, F 155

Jick, T   91
Johnson, G   31–33, *31, 32, 33*
Jolly, V   124

Kaplan, R S   *136*
Kay, J   40, 41
Kimmel, A J   74
Kirban, L   153
Koenig   74
   and four Cs: crisis, conflict,
      catastrophe and commerce
      74
Kotler, P   14,   74,   99, 108, 111, *112*
Kovacic, F M   55, 56, 57

Labov,   143
language consciousness levels   143
Larkin, J   56–57, 60
   and UK research audit   57
legislation (UK)
   Civil Contingencies Bill   54
   Copyright Designs and Patents Act
      (1988)   122
   Data Protection Act (1998)   88
   European   126
   Human Rights Act (1998)   91
Lerbinger, O   134
Liew, J   50
logos   76
Luftman, J N   21, 64
   data   21, *21*

Maathuis, O J M   78
McIlwee, T   90
Mackiewicz, A   72, 73
McMaster, M   42
McQuail, D   119–21
   and two-dimensional framework
      121
Macrae, C   73
management *see also* public relations
   (PR) strategy in management
   context
   extraordinary   35–36
   and implications of ordinary/
      extraordinary   37
   model of ordinary and extraordinary
      34

ordinary   35
   systems approach to   32–33
market intelligence   104–05, *105*
Marketing, Chartered Institute of (CIM)
   14, 101
marketing
   relationship   111
   strategic   102
marketing vs manufacturing   113–14
mass communication (as)   4, 119–22,
   121
   arena of public affairs   120
   benchmark to what is normal   12
   definitions of social reality   120
   power resource   120
   primary key to fame/celebrity status
      120
Mayer, M   73
measures and motives *see* research
   methods
media relations (and)   119–29
   campaign: Global Peace Index *see*
      main entry
   copyright   122
   global thinking, local action   124
   mass communication   119–21, *121*
      see also main entry
   media transparency   125
   message modelling   122–23 *see also*
      main entry
   personal vs social networking
      125–26
   rhetoric vs reality   121–22
message models   122–23
   publicity   123
   reception   123
   ritual or expressive   123
   transmission   122–23
Mexican Statement/definition   154
Meyer, R   *157*
Mintzberg, H   2
Mirdak, W   99
MobileEye   141
models
   communication management   57
   corporate communication academic
      6–10
   corporate identity   77

flexible firm 91
integrated marketing communication (IMC) mix 103, *104*
message *see also* message models
PR integration 6, *9*
Morgan, G 28
Moss-Kanter, R 91

National Health Service (NHS) 3, 155
Newman, W 73
Newspaper Licensing Agency (NLA), UK 122
Nijssen, E J 135, *136*
Nornes, R 40
Norton, D P *136*

Obama, B 140
O'Connell, B 60
Olaniran, B A 51–52
Oliver, S *8, 9, 28, 31, 39, 65, 91*
O'Neill, G 114
open systems theory 38
Open Work, The 76
operating and financial review (OFR) 43–44, *44*
organizational development 92
organizational paradigm 33–34
O'Sullivan, T 73, 77

Paul, G W 103
Pearce, J A II 15
perceptual mapping 104–05, *105*
PESTLE analysis 42
Petrash, G 45
pharmaceutical sector 138
Philadelphia Daily News 141
Pickton, D *104*
Pierce, C S 76
Pietersen, R 141
Porter, M (and) 104–07
  competitive advantage 106
  five competitive forces 104
  model 107
PricewaterhouseCoopers 137–38
public diplomacy 5
public opinion 16
Public Policy Research, UK Institute for 56

Public Relations, Chartered Institute of *see* CIPR
Public Relations Association, International 10, 16
public relations (PR) *see also* core governance
  integration model 6, *9*
  and organizational culture 6, *7, 8*
  vs propaganda 154–55
public relations (PR) strategy in management context (and) 1–26
  campaign: Nestlé 22–25 *see also main entry*
  control vs co-dependency 21, *21*
  corporate communication academic models 6–10
  diktat vs dialogue 5
  feedback cycle 20–21
  operational strategy 15–20, *17, 18–19*
  power and influence 4–5
  semantics 11–14

qualitative data analysis 137
Quinn, J B 45

reading behaviour 140–43
Regester, M 56–57, 60
Reich, R B 124
reflections/questions 25, 70, 86, 98, 118, 129, 151, 166
relationship marketing 111
relationships, theories of 4
Repper, F C 107
reputation and PR 11
reputation management (and) 71–86
  campaign: Electrotechnical University 'Leti' *see main entry*
  corporate identity 74–75
  corporate image 72–73
  image and branding 73–74
  logos and livery: semiotics 76–77 *see also* semiotics
  reputation indices 78–80, *79*
  substance vs style 77–78, *78*
  visual identity 75–76, *75*
research methods: measures and motives (and) 131–51

art vs science   132–33, *132*
balanced scorecard   135–36, *136*
campaign: Accenture, Germany *see main entry*
deconstruction guidelines   139
grounded theory   137–38
intertextuality analysis   144–46, *145, 146*
narrative methods   138
PR as social science   146–48
PR industry analysts   136–37
reading behaviour   140–44, *142, 143*
validity and reliability of   133–35, *135*
research/surveys (of/on)   10, 47, 55, 79–80
applied image   79
British trust in bankers (Gallup, 1986) 50
crises (1994)   57
eye-tracking   140–41, *142, 143*
lists – Mosaic   147
reading behaviour   140–41
risk (Aon, 2007)   40
risk management   40–41
risk models   40
Robinson, R B Jr   15
Rogers, C   72

sabotage   65
sales and marketing promotion (and) 99–118
business-to-business relations   108
campaign: Hitachi GST (Japan) *see main entry*
competitive advantage   104–07, *105, 106*
conceptual authenticity   100–01
customer relations   107–08
efficiency vs effectiveness   110–11
integrated marketing communication (IMC) mix model   103, *104*
knowledge and skill   101–03
marketing vs manufacturing   113–14
tools and techniques   111–13, *112, 113*
value-added   103–04 *see also main entry*

web analysis and evaluation 108–10, *109, 110*
sampling, random/non-random   147
Schlesinger, I A   36
Scholes, K   31–33, *31, 32, 33*
semiology   76
Shell and Brent Spar   120
Shuy, R W   143–44
Singer, P   77
small to medium-sized enterprises (SMEs)   3, 15
Smith, A   114
social networking   29, 125–26, 140
social performance indicators   80
software: SPSS for Windows   147–48
Sopow, E   56
Stacey, R D   34, 35–37
stakeholder(s)   11, 16, 62, 126
analysis   17
approach   146
groups   61–62
major   36
mapping   32, *32*
responsibilities   *18–19*
theory   16
Stanley, J   77
Steel, G R   41
Stein, B   91
strategic
alliances (Philips)   46–47, *46*
management   158
planning   38
PR   14, 34
strategies
global   124
Stuart, H   77
Sullivan, A J   134, 141
Susskind, L   56
sustainability   47

Target Group Index   106
Teece, D J   47
telecommunications   11
advances in   55–56
Texas Instruments   124
Thames Valley University Faculty of Professional Studies in London 50

theories of
  cognition and behaviour   4
  mass communication   4
  relationships   4
Thompson, J L   2
Thurow and conceptual framework of
    punctuated equilibrium   55
Toffler, A   101
Trade and Industry, Department of
    (UK)   61
Traeber, M   153
Turnbull, N   59
Turnbull Report   59–60
Turnbull Working Party 59
Twitter   140

United Kingdom (UK)
  Emergency Coordination Centre
      54
  Government Code of Conduct   41
  London Emergency Services Liaison
      Panel (LESLP)   54
United Nations Development
    Programme   158

value-added   103–04
  concepts   38
van den Bosch, A L M   76
van Riel, C B M   30, *30*, 78–79
Verbeke, A   134–35
Vienna Convention on Diplomatic
    Relations   5
vision, importance of   38

Wang, J   78
web analysis   126
  and evaluation   108–10, *109*, *110*
White, C   2
White, J   35, 37, 39
Williams, D E   51–52
Williams, H M   58
Wolfe, T   29
Wright, D   137

Y2K Regulation Fair Disclosure
    (Reg. FD)   61

Zerfass, A   136
Zhu, J H   55

ALSO AVAILABLE FROM KOGAN PAGE

PR IN PRACTICE SERIES

Effective Writing Skills for **Public Relations**

Fourth Edition

John Foster

ISBN: 978 0 7494 5109 7   Paperback   2008

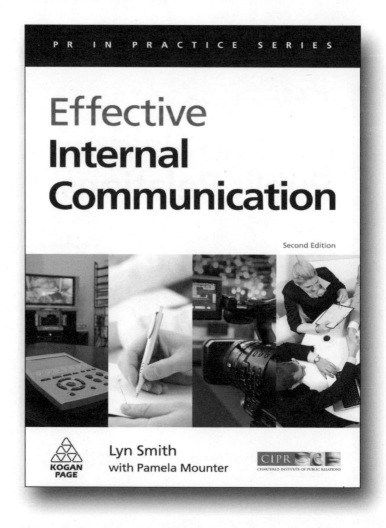